The Internal Triangle

The Internal Triangle

New Theories of Female Development

Lucy Holmes

JASON ARONSON
Lanham • Boulder • New York • Toronto • Plymouth, UK

Published in the United States of America
by Jason Aronson
An imprint of Rowman & Littlefield Publishers, Inc.
A wholly owned subsidiary of The Rowman & Littlefield Publishing Group, Inc.
4501 Forbes Boulevard, Suite 200, Lanham, Maryland 20706
www.rowmanlittlefield.com

Estover Road, Plymouth PL6 7PY, United Kingdom

British Library Cataloguing in Publication Information Available

Library of Congress Cataloging-in-Publication Data Available

ISBN-13: 978-0-7657-0549-5 (cloth: alk. paper)
ISBN-10: 0-7657-0549-4 (cloth: alk. paper)
ISBN-13: 978-0-7657-0550-1 (pbk.: alk. paper)
ISBN-10: 0-7657-0550-8 (pbk.: alk. paper)

Printed in the United States of America

∞™ The paper used in this publication meets the minimum requirements of American National Standard for Information Sciences—Permanence of Paper for Printed Library Materials, ANSI/NISO Z39.48-1992.

For Eleanor and Peter Johnson,
who changed my mind

Contents

Acknowledgments

For permission to reprint material for which they hold copyright, grateful acknowledgment is made to the following sources:

Chapter 1: "The Internal Triangle: New Theories of Female Development." *Modern Psychoanalysis* 25, no. 2 (2000): 207–26.

Chapter 2: "The Object Within: Childbirth as a Developmental Milestone." *Modern Psychoanalysis* 25, no. 1 (2000): 109–34.

Chapter 5: "Women in Group and Women's Groups." *International Journal of Group Psychotherapy* 52, no. 2 (2002): 171–88.

Chapter 7: "Hell Hath No Fury: How Women Get Even." *Modern Psychoanalysis* 29, no. 1 (2004): 49–61.

Introduction

It is ironic that, despite the fact that the majority of human beings involved in psychoanalysis today, both analysts and patients, are women, many aspects of feminine psychosexual development remain what Freud (1926, 212) described as a "dark continent." The history of psychoanalytic theory has been dominated by a tendency to see human development as male development. Women, for the most part, have been viewed in psychoanalysis as "a catalogue of lacks" (Benjamin 1988, 94).

Beginning in 1908 with his first mention of penis envy in "On the Sexual Theories of Children," Freud always focused his hypotheses about the feminine character on a female deficiency in relation to the male: envy of the penis, he consistently asserted, is the engine that drives little girls on their difficult journey toward becoming feminine women.

Almost one hundred years after Freud started writing about women, theories of female development and character still center on, or at least wrestle with, penis envy. In the 1970s and 1980s, the concept was reframed by feminist psychoanalysts in a way that considers the enormous importance for both sexes of the pre-Oedipal mother—that powerful and abundant female figure of our infancy that gives the lie to feminine deficiency. According to writers like Nancy Chodorow and Jessica Benjamin, little girls envy the male genital because they see it as a ticket out of the symbiotic merging with the early mother that all human children eventually want to escape. Little boys, with their protruding sexual organ, are so clearly "not my mother" that their path from infancy toward separation and individuation is infinitely easier than the little girl's, who like mother has "nothing," where her brother has "something."

The concept of penis envy, though usually irritating to women, even women psychoanalysts, is borne out again and again in the analysis of female patients and in the clinical observation of three-year-old girls at play. The theory that the penis facilitates independence from the engulfing mother of infancy adds complexity to the concept in an interesting and helpful way, but is envy of the phallus all there is to know about female development?

Even after reluctantly accepting the concept of penis envy as I proceeded through my own analysis and analytic training, I didn't give these matters much thought until much later. My interest in female development took a circuitous route through two important milestones in my own life—the birth of my two children.

When my first child was born in 1979, I was well into my personal psychoanalysis; by the time my second child arrived in 1985, I was studying at an institute with the goal of becoming an analyst myself. I found the experiences of pregnancy and childbirth to be profound in ways I didn't totally understand at the time of my first child's birth, a highly technological experience in a big-city hospital. After giving birth to my second child at a freestanding birth center in a family-focused environment, I realized that the childbirth experience had changed me in a dramatic way. I found myself with a different mind than the one I had had before I conceived. I began to have the idea, really just an unfocused intuition at the time, that pregnancy and childbirth were milestones in a woman's development; that is to say, that, as in adolescence, a person comes out of the experience deeply altered.

When I began my doctoral work, I decided that I wanted to do psychoanalytic research on pregnant women to see what I could learn about this idea. I formed two groups of women, one in my private practice in New York City, the other in the OB/GYN clinic of an inner-city hospital. The groups consisted of women who considered pregnancy a "burning issue." They were pregnant, or infertile and unhappy about it, or conflicted about bearing a child. For two years, I listened to these groups of women to see if I could develop hypotheses about the unconscious meaning of birth.

The first thing that struck me was the sense of all the ghosts in the treatment room. The women were there in the sessions, but so were their mothers and their fathers. Women consistently experienced pregnancy as "becoming my mother," and if this idea was too repellant, they were often infertile. If a woman had made a stronger identification with father than with mother, she often verbalized ambivalence about pregnancy or sometimes noted a conscious refusal to consider bearing a child. If a woman was already pregnant, her fetus was definitely there in the room too, usually as an object of projection. The unborn baby was alternately experienced like another object in a woman's life, or as an aspect of the self. If a parent had been perceived as ruthless or parasitic, the fetus was often experienced as feeding on its mother in a way which would destroy her. If a woman suffered from a lack of self-esteem, she frequently was convinced that her baby was defective or deformed, like the devalued self. When the unborn baby was the object of love from the mother, it was seen as the mother's own best self, her ego ideal.

Bollas (1992, 56) wrote about "the ghosts within us," the internal objects that influence us. He described these internal objects as highly condensed psychic textures, the traces of our encounters with the object world (59). Listening to how the themes played out in different ways in the minds of the women I worked with, I began to speculate that there is a strong tendency in women to internalize parental objects. All these women in their own unique ways seemed to be dealing, on a fantasy level, with an internal triangle of mother, father, and self. I listened over and over as a drama involving these three intrapsychic characters unfolded within each woman, according to a script of her own creation. I also saw that the object within, the unborn baby, became the receptacle for all the projected fantasies involving this script. Even more interesting to me was the fact that, as the women began to give birth, there was a significant shift in the internal triangle. Once subordinated to the internalized maternal and paternal imagoes, the female self gained significant ego strength in the process of birth, especially if the experience was not masked by drugs and technology. I saw again and again that enormous psychic development occurred when the fetus, so often the focus of the internal drama, was pushed out into the world. This transition from inner fantasy world to outer reality consistently gave women a sense of empowerment. The infant, the repository of so many primitive fantasies and projections, could now be seen, held, controlled, and nurtured. In this triumphant transition, the mother's ego was greatly strengthened.

It was at this point, when I had hypothesized an internal triangle that is characteristic of the female mind, that I began to reconsider female development. Psychoanalytic theory, by and large, offered no account of the psychosexual development of women other than a negative one: Little girls don't have penises and that is sufficient explanation for how human beings become feminine. But is a lack of a phallus enough to explain the complexity of femininity? Freud and later psychoanalytic theorists have associated attributes both negative and positive with the female character. Women, we are told, are more narcissistic, passive, and masochistic than men (Deutsch 1944; 1945). They have weaker superegos than the male sex and are much more interested in being loved than loving. They are generally unfit for psychoanalysis, because the rigors of female development leave them no energy for psychic reconfiguration (Freud 1931; 1932; 1933). Feminine human beings tend to be more empathetic than men and they strive for connection with others (Miller 1976). Their moral code is never as rigid or as dualistic as male human beings; issues of right and wrong are always determined in an atmosphere of complexity and in consideration of the realities of all the people involved in an issue (Gilligan 1982). Can all of these dynamics be explained by a phallocentric focus on the human genitals?

I began to be convinced that there was more to say about female development, and I hypothesized that what I called the *internal triangle* played a part in that development. I became interested in how and why little girls tend to internalize parental figures in such a vivid way. Relying on the work of Freud, Melanie Klein, Blos, and other writers who had focused on pre-Oedipal and Oedipal issues, as well as adolescent development, I formulated a theory.

The internal triangle characteristic of women is a unique solution to the problem of being a deficient "little man" (Freud 1932, 118). With no manifest representation of a difference from the powerful mother of infancy, little girls on a fantasy level incorporate the maternal object—and this fantasy "mother in me" offers the girl a sense of mastery and control over the engulfing mother of the preverbal period. When faced with the humiliations of the Oedipal period, the female child again uses introjection to internalize the father. The reason for this is again to gain mastery and control over an essentially uncontrollable object. The introjection of the father gives the little girl the power of the phallus on a fantasy level, but it also serves another function. The internalization of the paternal imago has the added benefit of subordinating and subduing the powerful maternal introject. Within the complex endopsychic feminine world, girls freely discharge both libido and aggression toward internalized objects.

The theory of the internal triangle, like all psychoanalytic theories, cannot be proven using the qualitative techniques of traditional science and the laboratory (though neuroscientists today are observing structures and systems in the human brain that seem to validate many of Freud's original theories). Knowledge of unconscious processes in analysis is always inferential, but we need not denigrate analytic theory because of it. The scientific study of the external world is also often inferential: Scientists discovered germs before they could actually see them through a microscope by making inferences about what was making people sick, and then experimenting with those inferences to see if they were useful in helping people stay well or recover when they were sick.

How do psychoanalysts judge whether a theory is a good one? Nigel Mackay (1989), who has written extensively about psychoanalytic motivation and explanation, believes that we determine the value of a theory by its ability to explain the facts well. We develop a theory by listening to what our patients actually say; then we study, moving forward, whether what they say confirms or discredits our theory. If the theory helps us explain our patients' behaviors, if it allows us to make predictions about future behaviors which prove to be accurate, then we can judge the theory to be a good one. Good theoretical constructs help the analyst to organize and give meaning to diverse clinical data that initially appear unrelated. When a theory is useful, it permits a space-time continuity between past causes and current behavior. In short, good theories help us understand our patients.

The theories of penis envy and the Oedipal conflict, for example, have proven to be excellent ones because they are confirmed over and over in play therapy with children and by the actual words spoken by adult analytic patients. They also help us explain the unconscious meaning of many phenomena of human interaction. The concept of penis envy enriches our understanding of adolescent tomboys and female overachievers and, more importantly, the almost universal devaluation of "the second sex" (de Beauvoir 1952). Oedipal theory gives us insight into why so many men "marry their mothers" and why fathers often feel that their sons-in-law are not "good enough" for their daughters. Ever since Freud first formulated these ideas, they have been helpful in understanding and predicting behavior.

In the ten years since I first developed my theories of female development, I have worked with women in all phases of their lives, from adolescence to old age. The theory of the internal triangle has been confirmed over and over by what women actually say to me and has helped me understand the challenges that female human beings face in every phase of life.

Female development is experienced in flesh and blood; every developmental event uncompromisingly marks a woman's corporeal being and stirs up archaic feelings (Montgrain 1983). Women have three developmental crises that manifest themselves in the body in dramatic ways. These three events—the flow of blood at the onset of menstruation in adolescence, the swelling of the body in pregnancy, and the cessation of the menses at menopause—indicate to the female human being, in a way impossible to ignore, that she is changing. The onset of menstruation signals that she will never be a child again; the belly of pregnancy, that she will never be truly alone in her narcissism again; and the climacteric, that she must grow old and die (Bibring 1961). Rooted in physicality, all of these turning points lead to intense psychic disequilibrium, and each crisis is characterized by a confrontation with the internal triangle, which is constantly being confronted and reconfigured. In favorable circumstances, each of these developmental milestones can facilitate steps toward maturity and higher functioning. In pathology, they can lead to depression and despair.

This book is an attempt to enrich the theory about female development in a way that focuses on women, not on the ways they are different from men. Chapter 1 describes an internal triangle of maternal imago, paternal imago, and self, which is unique to female development. Girls are "organless" and, because they can neither suckle their mothers nor penetrate their fathers, they gain control by introjecting both parental objects. The introjection of the pre-Oedipal mother is a primitive incorporation, an oral pre-identification in which mother is ingested with her milk. The internalization of the Oedipal father is more highly evolved, and is a relationship to, as well as a mental representation of, the object. After the relative quiet of the latency period, female adolescence is characterized by a surge in intensity of both libido and aggression toward internalized objects.

Chapter 2 focuses on childbirth as a developmental milestone in a woman's life. Pregnancy and childbirth constitute a crisis in the life cycle out of which, in favorable circumstances, new psychic structures are created and mental functioning is integrated. Using the techniques of modern psychoanalytic research, I discuss themes and unconscious associations regarding childbirth, gathered from data collected in my years of work with two groups of pregnant women. The complexity of the female endopsychic world is emphasized. Specifically, pregnancy can facilitate a restructuring of the psychic triangle of internalized maternal and paternal objects and self in a way that has a maturational effect. The self gains new authority in relationship to these internalized objects. Existing psychoanalytic literature on childbirth is reviewed, and a case is presented of a pregnant woman that demonstrates exactly how issues of "masculine" and "feminine" identification become truly integrated in pregnancy and childbirth.

Chapter 3 describes the emergence of the self that can occur as a positive aspect of menopause. Internalized objects, which have been so helpful to female development, tend to be expelled out of the psyche in an anal-sadistic burst of psychic housecleaning at the climacteric. The fantasy of psychic "emptiness" so common in menopausal women reflects this expulsion. Associated both in the unconscious and the culture as a rehearsal for death, menopause presents a crisis for survival, that, in favorable circumstances, can initiate a new period of creativity and vigor; in pathology, it can result in a passive hopelessness. Loss of reproductive function is a symbolic castration which unconsciously reactivates the rage at the mother that initiated the female Oedipal conflict. This results in a renewed unconscious desire to identify with the father and a victory of more masculine traits, such as aggression and assertiveness, over the feminine qualities of passivity and empathy. The ascendancy of the self over the myriad and complex introjections and identifications of the female psyche is the emotional goal of menopause. Old age provides another opportunity to work through the issues of infancy and the relationship with the pre-Oedipal mother.

Chapter 4 is an attempt to answer Freud's classic question, "What does woman want?" The women I have worked with, both individually and in groups, want to be able to use their empathy and intuition in the service of their own egos. They want the feminine tendency to identify to be a tool, not a prison. The internal triangle, though it solves the problem of separating from and still identifying with an object, also sets the stage for the female ego to be totally dominated by its own identifications. The subjugation that women experience from *within* is infinitely more insidious than their subordination to a masculine culture. Because the intrapsychic coercion is largely unconscious and established at a time when the female ego is still young and fragile, women cannot deal with this oppression in a realistic manner. Projecting the internalized object onto the analyst sets the stage for feelings *toward*, not *with* the parental imago. Likewise, the projection of this imago *into* the analyst for "protection" frees the budding ego to emerge. By recognizing and accepting these projections, the analyst can help the patient approach the internalized object playfully, molding and shaping it into a more elastic, less rigid imago.

Chapter 5 delineates some of the special issues involved in treating women in group or leading women's groups. Since female development is characterized by the introjection of maternal and paternal objects—creating a rich internal world for women—the feminine tendency to become diffused in identifications sometimes results in women feeling overpowered in mixed-gender groups. I advocate women's groups for the traditionally "feminine" woman, that is, the woman who has a rather impoverished sense of self in terms of her internalized objects. Women's groups are also helpful during adolescence, pregnancy, and menopause, milestones of female development, because these are times when women are in profound crisis and may find it difficult to speak about these quintessentially feminine events in the presence of men.

The use of play in women's groups is the subject of chapter 6. As young girls develop, their play progresses from narcissism to object relatedness. This progression is usually reflected in group therapy. Early in treatment, a patient usually wants to play alone. She has a "story" to relate, usually focusing on the way the world and the people in it have been a source of disappointment or pain. She wants to play with her story/toy with very little awareness that there are other potential playmates in the room. Early on in a group, the analyst is perceived not as a real and separate object but as a toy to be used. As the group matures and members become more object-oriented, the analyst and the group can together create a third party in the analysis, which is the play space between them. Group members play with the analyst by projecting early objects onto and into her. The analyst identifies and attempts to understand these projections but does so, inevitably, through the filter of her own subjective experience. The fluid process of lively interchange between the inner and the outer worlds, and the continual bounce of projective and introjective identifications, liberate feelings and help patients say new things.

Women are not only very good at play but they are also excellent at revenge. In chapter 7, I discuss three ways that women get even in a uniquely feminine way, both inside and outside the treatment room: by suffering, by seduction, and by repeating an unconscious identification. I present several clinical examples of aggressive suffering, as well as a patient who got even by symbolically seducing her analyst and breaking her heart. Finally, I describe a particularly malevolent case of revenge carried out in a woman's group using repetition and unconscious identification with a cruel father. All three methods have major drawbacks, so I conclude with some more constructive ways of getting even.

Chapter 8 focuses on a concept I call the "mind of the mother." Patients frequently demonstrate repetitive, rigid ways of thinking, believing, and acting which have very little to do with reality. One patient called this "living in the mind of my mother." Living in the mind of the mother is set down in the earliest stages of life, long before there is any awareness of an object perceived as separate from the self. Being trapped in the mother's mind feels "cellular," because the cells of the fetus were literally formed out of the soma and psyche of the mother. When we are in "the mind of the mother," libido is expressed in the unconscious identification with the mother, and aggression is projected into the mother and then turned against the self. In the here and now of the session, patients repeat preverbal experience that was, is now, and will always be the way the patient sees and deals with the world. Patients want to change their feelings in analysis but this doesn't usually happen. Instead, the patient changes her mind. The feelings are the expression of the mind of the mother, the earliest impressions created at a cellular level and mistaken from that time forward for reality. Giving them up would mean coming apart, mentally and probably physically.

Woman's whole psychosexual development, from conception to old age, could be described as a confrontation with the internalized mother, both the powerful pre-Oedipal mother and the "castrated" Oedipal mother who submits to father. From the formation of subjective reality out of the "mind of the mother," through the first attempts to separate from the pre-Oedipal mother that initiate the formation of the internal triangle, and to the practically universal cry of despair of elderly women when they tell me, "I look in the mirror and see my mother!" women have a unique challenge. They walk a tightrope between identifying with and separating from the mother who feeds; the mother who bleeds, conceives, and gives birth; and the mother who ages and dies. This elaborate feminine dance between libido and aggression in relation to the internalized mother defines female development in a much more profound way than penis envy—and the choreography of that dance is the subject of this book.

CHAPTER ONE

The Internal Triangle: New Theories of Female Development

Psychoanalysis has historically viewed human development as male development. A penis, or the lack of one, has been seen as the engine that drives human beings from the polymorphously perverse sexuality of infancy to fully formed adult identity as a male or female. Femininity, with all its complexities, has been explained by the fact that in this world, woman functions as the deficient "Other" (de Beauvoir 1952).

In the last thirty years, feminist psychoanalysts have attempted to address the integrity rather than the "difference" of female maturation and development, but many attempts at a new theory have a basis more in sociology, anthropology, and politics than psychoanalysis. Much of this literature borrows heavily from the school of object-relations theory in addressing the feminine need for "connection" and the importance of issues of boundaries and merging for women. But almost one hundred years after the creation of psychoanalysis, a coherent theory of female development, based on the cornerstones of the unconscious and drive theory, has yet to be formulated.

Freud was a male genius and psychoanalysis has traditionally been a phallocentric theory. Freud himself acknowledged that his theories of femininity were "incomplete and fragmentary" (Freud 1932, 135). Freud never answered his question to Marie Bonaparte, "What does woman want?" to his own satisfaction, but the body of work he did leave on femininity provides a starting point for a discussion of the psychology of women.

Freud asserted that an important sexual theory of children is that there is only one genital, and that the genital is male (Freud 1905). The penis and clitoris can be seen, while the ovaries and womb cannot, and small children react to this fact by assuming that the boy's penis is "bigger and better" than the girl's clitoris, and that she therefore functions as a "little man" (Freud 1933, 118). At about the age of four, the boy realizes that girls are missing a penis, and at about the same time, the girl realizes she is missing one, too.

This painful discovery that boys have something where she has "nothing" initiates the girl's Oedipal conflict. She develops penis envy and hates her formerly beloved mother for the fact of their mutual castration, and so she turns to her father with the incestuous wish that he give her a child. Freud saw this wish for a child as a displaced longing for a penis (Freud 1924).

Because a girl's castration has already occurred and can no longer be feared, girls don't experience the dramatic destruction of the Oedipus complex typical of boys. This has several consequences, according to Freud. One is that the Oedipus conflict in girls disappears or becomes repressed much more slowly, and in fact may persist throughout a woman's life. Another consequence is the relative weakness of the superego in women. Freud attributed a larger amount of narcissism to women, asserting that they need to be loved far more than they need to love.

In "Female Sexuality," Freud discussed the importance of the pre-Oedipal period for girls. The female reaches the Oedipus complex only after a long and intense attachment to her mother. Both boys and girls develop hatred for the pre-Oedipal mother for many reasons, but boys can displace their hatred onto their fathers as rival; girls are necessarily more ambivalent. When a girl turns away from her mother in favor of the father, there is a marked reduction of active sexual impulses in favor of passive ones (Freud 1931). Freud equated *activity* with masculinity and *passivity* with femininity. But he went on to say that every individual is a mixture of masculine and feminine characteristics and that, often, much activity is required to achieve passive aims. The suppression of women's aggression—which is prescribed for them constitutionally and imposed on them socially—favors the development of masochism and therefore Freud saw masochism as truly feminine (Freud 1932).

Helene Deutsch (1944) wrote about a "feminine core," the foundation of the feminine personality, which is characterized by three essential traits: narcissism, passivity, and masochism. Female passivity, according to Deutsch, is activity turned inward. Girls, like boys, have active aggressive and sexual impulses, but because the clitoris is unable to gratify these impulses as effectively as the penis, the little girl inhibits her aggressive activity and turns toward a passive-receptive style of functioning more suited to the vagina.

Like passivity, masochism is the outcome of a mechanism of instinctual reversal that turns inward the energies that are directed toward the outer world.

Passive drives of the ego are connected in both boys and girls to the mother, while activity and reality are centered on the figure of the father. But the father is more supportive of his son's drive toward activity and aggression than his daughter's, and so the girl encounters an inhibition of her ego development imposed by the outside world. The girl gives up her aggression and is offered a bribe for her sacrifice, the love and tenderness of the father. The renounced aggressive impulses are turned around to passivity and they endow the passive state of being loved with a masochistic character. Feminine masochism, unlike moral masochism, which is characterized by guilt and self-punishment, is based upon the active impulse of a healthy ego to adjust to reality.

Narcissism serves as a counterweight to masochism in the feminine woman and guards the ego from passive-masochistic decline. Healthy narcissism, the libido's taking of the ego for its object, protects the female personality from the dangers of the sometimes masochistic sexual goals of her reproductive functioning. The distribution of forces between the narcissistic ego and feminine masochism allows a sublimation of sexuality into eroticism—which is uniquely feminine. The interplay of passivity, masochism, and narcissism is responsible for many positive feminine attributes: the enormous capacity for identification with objects, the rich inner life of fantasy and imagination, the ability to sacrifice self for a higher goal, and the tendency toward intuition (Deutsch 1944).

Ernest Jones, Karen Horney, and Marie Bonaparte were other early theorists who devoted large parts of their careers to the study of female psychology. Bonaparte, a drive theorist like Freud and Deutsch, believed that women are constitutionally and biologically bisexual, and for her, the central problem in feminine development was the masculinity complex. She saw the clitoris as an unsatisfactory little penis and insisted that women have less aggression and libido than men (Bonaparte 1951).

Jones and Horney disagreed with Freud about several important aspects of female functioning. Jones asserted that femininity is innate, and that the masculinity little girls demonstrate is defensive. The vagina that Freud had asserted was "undiscovered" in childhood, Jones saw as "denied." Rather than emphasizing penis envy, he felt girls have an interest, from a very early age, in the inside rather than the outside of their bodies. Jones also differed with Freud about the clitoris. He saw the clitoris as part of the female organ, not as a deficient substitute for the penis. He maintained that the wish to have a child is not a displacement of the wish for a penis, but a true feminine wish (Jones 1927; 1935).

Horney (1967), who agreed with most of Jones's ideas, was a great advocate of the influence of culture and society on feminine development. According to Horney, penis envy, the masculinity complex, and female masochism were not rooted in the anatomical-physiological-psychic characteristics of females, but must be considered in the context of social organizations that oppress women. She argued that genital differences had been emphasized in analytic theory, while the great biological differences, namely the different parts played by men and women in the functions of reproduction, had been totally overlooked. Though agreeing that penis envy is "an inevitable phenomenon in the life of female children," Horney asserted that women have in motherhood an indisputable and by no means negligible physiological superiority. Because girls have no external sex organ and don't come into their true sexual powers until adulthood, they are literally "in the dark" about their later superiority (Horney 1967, 66).

The work of Jones, Horney, and Bonaparte left us with more questions than answers about several controversies in the theory of feminine development. The debates are still raging about whether femininity is innate or acquired, whether penis envy is anatomically or culturally grounded, whether the vagina is undiscovered or denied in early childhood, and whether men have inherently stronger drives than women. If we accept the most basic tenets of psychoanalysis, the first question seems to be the easiest on which to take a position. Freud rested his entire body of work on the concept that human beings are not born, they are made. The most fundamental idea of psychoanalysis is that it takes enormous effort to become logical, ethical, and civilized. Though most of us achieve an unstable victory over the primitive unconscious, it is with us all our lives. Acknowledging that the journey from animal to human being is a struggle demands that we concede that femininity is no more innate than rationality or morality. Psychoanalysis insists that they must be explained to be understood.

Horney's cultural perspective on penis envy cannot be totally discounted, though it is perhaps fair to say that, in any study of human development, drives are primary and precede culture. Ego is formed when sexual and aggressive instincts confront reality and adapt themselves to it, and sexist culture is certainly real. The passivity, masochism, and narcissism that Deutsch described can be seen as adaptations that female human beings have to make to live as women in the world. But there is an inherent danger in Horney's emphasis on culture to explain femininity. If sexist culture is given full responsibility for the difficulties of becoming female, it is easy to overlook the role that the primary thinking of the unconscious plays in making sexism seem like "second nature." Women's universal subordination can only be understood by an exploration of the early interplay of libido and aggression in very young girls, which sets up a situation in which subordination is the best solution to a uniquely feminine problem. Passivity and masochism are sexual and aggressive instincts, originally directed at the outer world, turned inward; this seems to be a classic example of a drive meeting the reality principle, which in this case is not only society's demand that little girls be "feminine" but also, on an intrapsychic level, the demand that drives originally directed toward objects be turned back onto self and internalized objects. Like the aggression and activity that are masculine drive derivatives, passivity and masochism are only "bad" if they function purely in the service of the death instinct, unmitigated by Eros, the life instinct.

The question of awareness of the vagina is closely related to whether femininity is acquired or innate. Certainly, if girls are born feminine, then it is likely that consciousness of the vagina is there from the beginning. Clinically, this is a question that is almost impossible to answer with any certainty. Both boys and girls experience the pleasure of the fullness of a passive organ (the sphincter) in the anal period. Bonaparte contended that girls passively cathect the cloaca (the vagina and anus coenesthetically combined), and that this cathexis becomes the prototype for later vaginal functioning (Bonaparte 1951). Freud's idea that the erotogenicity of the clitoris is replaced by the vagina has been disputed by more modern theorists. Women never relinquish the clitoris as an erotogenic zone; the vagina is an addition to their sexual pleasure, not a replacement, and this anatomical complexity reflects the psychic intricacy of women.

Just as difficult to prove is the idea that drives are stronger in men than in women. Given the immense diversity of human beings and a world that includes plenty of aggressive women and passive men, it is hard to accept Bonaparte's theory as inevitable. What is clearer is that the culture that Horney felt was so important, as well as the modifications of the sexual and aggressive instincts in female development, dictates that male human beings have more permission to be aggressive and active, while women are expected to be loving and passive. This means that the vicissitudes of the drives are more complex in women than men, and so they must erect more defenses against them. As Deutsch and Freud reminded us, it takes a tremendous amount of psychic activity to become passive in a way acceptable to both ego and id.

Horney felt that woman envy on the part of man is psychogenetically older and therefore more fundamental than penis envy (Horney 1967). Given the developmental sequence which Horney herself confirms with her statement about little girls being in the dark about their sexual powers until the vagina and womb are discovered, this at first seems unlikely. The superiority of the phallus is a phenomenon of early childhood; the womb doesn't come into its own until much later. But Horney's theory of the primacy of woman envy becomes logical when we consider that for both boys and girls, woman is the original, omnipotent source of life. In the earliest stages of human existence, what Freud called the oral period, the organs of activity are the breasts, and all human beings, male and female, take the passive "feminine" position of receiving in relation to their mothers. It is in the first perception by the infant that the breast is not a part of itself, but a separate object attached to a powerful Other with her own subjectivity not under its control, that woman envy is born in every human being, whether male or female.

Modern analysis has emphasized the profound importance of the pre-Oedipal period for both boys and girls (Ernsberger 1976). For both sexes, the infant's first symbiotic relationship is with a woman, and in that relationship, the woman is not castrated, but phallic and powerful. Her breasts, the part-objects which introduce the baby to the world, are protruding organs of activity and penetration, the source of life. To the suckling child, whether male or female, the woman is primally omnipotent, and the child is passive in relation to her.

Melanie Klein was one of the first theorists to address the significance of this universal situation. She emphasized the constant interaction between love and hate in this pre-relationship. The baby's mother is both desired and hated with all the strength and intensity that are characteristic of the primitive urges of the infant. The mother as the "good breast" satisfies all the baby's cravings and makes her feel secure, but she can also frustrate. These inevitable frustrations create destructive fantasies in the baby, and these fantasies feel like death wishes, in that the baby may feel that she has really destroyed the mother with her hate and is going on destroying her. This has extremely important consequences for the mind, according to Klein. Feelings of guilt and distress now enter as a new element in the emotion of love. A pressing urge to make sacrifices develops, in order to put things right and help loved people who have been harmed in fantasy. We acquire a capacity to identify with those we love, to put ourselves in their place (Klein and Riviere 1964).

The interplay between primitive love and hate during the oral stage, which Klein described, sets the stage for the child's first primitive identification with its mother. With the ingestion of milk, the infant, more or less on the level of fantasy, incorporates the powerful mother into herself and keeps her inside her body. This incorporation of the mother is driven by both libido and aggression and is both a wish to take the mother in and to destroy her. This "mother-in-me" is particularly strong in female infants, for reasons that Nancy Chodorow would elaborate on later, but it is important to consider that the first introjection is of an active, phallic mother. When the primitive aggression that Freud and Klein maintained is inevitable in the first relationship asserts itself, boys are much better equipped than girls to oppose the maternal object because they have a penis.

Later feminist psychoanalysts were to point out the importance for both sexes of the drive to separate from maternal engulfment and to frame penis envy in terms of the phallus as a symbol of separation from maternal omnipotence. This drive to oppose maternal omnipotence is fueled by the libido's love for the world and also by the inevitable aggression toward the mother. Klein provided an important contribution to the importance of early introjects and identifications in girls. The little girl's aggression toward her mother, first experienced in the oral stage as a wish to "eat her up," thereby replacing her, later develops into a deep resentment over the manifest evidence of their mutual anatomical deficiency. The girl feels guilty and conflicted about her wish to destroy her mother and she develops a wish to make reparation, which is expressed as a capacity to identify with her mother. The early incorporation of the powerful maternal object redirects inward the sexual and aggressive impulses originally focused outward toward the mother. It is because of the psychic space created by the incorporated mother, the "mother-in-me," that little girls become interested in the inside rather than the outside. Girls focus inward at a very early age, as Jones suggested, because of the specific challenges, unique to females, that they face in the pre-Oedipal and Oedipal periods. The tendency to internalize objects, more pronounced in girls than boys, sets up a rich, endopsychic world in females.

Crowell emphasized that girls and boys have very different experiences in the pre-Oedipal and Oedipal periods, because girls are mothered by an object of the same sex while boys are not (Crowell 1981). Nancy Chodorow, another feminist psychoanalyst, theorized that sons are objects for their mothers, while daughters are more likely to be experienced in narcissistic "oneness." Girls experience themselves as the self of the mother's fantasy, while boys become the Other. Because women are more likely to experience their daughters in this narcissistic oneness, the pre-Oedipal period is longer and more intense in girls than in boys, and women are more likely to experience boundary confusion and a lack of a sense of separateness from the world.

Girls enter the triangular Oedipal situation later and they never completely renounce pre-Oedipal issues. The turn toward the father becomes a symbol of freedom from the dependence on and merging with the pre-Oedipal mother. The Oedipal girl's rejection of her mother is a defense against primary identification, hence her own internal affair as much as a relational affair in the world.

The female Oedipal complex is triangular in a way the boy's is not. Fathers do not become the sort of emotionally exclusive Oedipal object for girls that mothers do for boys. For girls, there is no absolute change of object, and this means that there is no single Oedipal mode or quick resolution of the conflict. Girls cannot and do not reject their mothers and women in favor of their fathers and men. They remain in a bisexual triangle throughout childhood and into puberty—and though they usually make a sexual resolution in favor of men, they retain an internal emotional triangle throughout life.

Chodorow described penis envy as the symbolic expression of the wish to detach from the mother and become autonomous rather than as a wish to be a man. A daughter does not have the different and desirable penis the son possesses to oppose maternal omnipotence, and she sees the father's penis as a symbol of independence and separateness from the mother. Chodorow saw Freud's notion that there is only one genital which people either have or are missing as a way the child defends himself psychologically against the overwhelming importance of its early mother image.

Girls do not define themselves in terms of the renunciation of pre-Oedipal relational modes to the extent that boys do, so regression to these modes feels less threatening to women than to men. From the retention of pre-Oedipal attachments to their mothers, girls come to define and experience themselves as continuous with others. An ambivalent struggle for a sense of separateness and independence from mother, an emotional, if not erotic, bisexual oscillation between mother and father, and "mother–child" and "male–female" issues are themes throughout the female life cycle (Chodorow 1978).

Chodorow is an object-relations theorist, but her ideas reveal the most basic problem for women, which is a problem concerning the drives, and it is this: How does a human being direct the healthy aggression needed to separate from an object with which they are originally merged in narcissistic oneness and with which they must identify if they are to achieve maturation as a female? The solution to this problem requires an integration and fusion of the life and death instincts which is unique to females.

Jessica Benjamin (1988) addressed this paradoxical requirement for women, that they must simultaneously separate from and identify with, their mothers. Both boys and girls use the father to achieve separation from the mother, but the boy has a simpler path. His aggression toward his mother, which is experienced as dangerous by both sexes, can be projected onto his father during his Oedipal complex—and when that complex is shattered, he can deny and devalue his connection to his mother by achieving male identification with his father. The girl cannot disrupt her primitive symbiosis with mother by using male identification to revolt against it. More important, the turning away of the girl from mother to father is problematic because—given the fact that most relationships between mothers and fathers are still permeated with inequality and subtle sexism—girls risk exchanging symbiosis for domination and control when they turn to their fathers. Fathers, because of the disidentification with women that their own Oedipal periods required, cannot see their daughters as they do their sons. They tend to unconsciously treat girls as nascent sex objects rather than subjects in their own right. Therefore, the use of the father to separate from the mother sets up the split, so common in women, between autonomy and sexuality. Little girls cannot use their connections to the Oedipal father defensively to deny their dependence on mother, nor constructively to forge a sense of separate selfhood. When her turn toward the father ends in frustration, the little girl redirects her desires, both sexual and aggressive, back toward herself, creating the passivity and masochism described by Deutsch and the muting of both libido and aggression delineated by Bonaparte.

Benjamin, like Chodorow, saw penis envy as a symbol of revolt and separation from omnipotent maternal power. She cites French analyst Janine Chasseguet-Smirgel, who demonstrated that Freud's description of women as castrated and powerless is the exact opposite of a small child's unconscious image of the mother (Chasseguet-Smirgel 1970). So, it becomes clear that penis envy itself goes through vicissitudes in the rocky road of feminine development. Beginning in the manifest, primitive awareness that boys have one more appendage than girls, which inspires a childish outrage not unlike the indignation when the cookie is unevenly divided around the nursery school table, it develops into a desire for the father's phallus, which represents a fantasy of escape from engulfment by the omnipotent, phallic mother, and finally becomes entrenched in the humiliation of the Oedipal failure. The father's sexual rejection of his daughter is not as traumatic for female development as his refusal of her identification with his idealized autonomy and sexuality represented by the penis. The defeated little girl's "lack," expressed symbolically in penis envy, is the gap left in her subjectivity by the rejecting father (Benjamin 1988) and the return to female identification.

Chodorow and Benjamin both focused on the pre-Oedipal period in females, expanding on Freud's conviction that this period is crucial for girls. Infants of both sexes are originally merged in narcissistic oneness with mother, but boys have a path out of this symbiosis that is not open to girls. The boy's penis is manifest anatomical evidence of his separateness from mother. He clearly possesses something that the omnipotent mother does not, and he uses his gender identification with his father to devalue maternal power and deny his "mother-in-me." This defensive devaluation and denial is why his Oedipal conflict is literally "smashed to pieces" (Freud 1925, 257). What is totally obliterated in the boy is the maternal introject and, in this act of psychic violence, male chauvinism and domination is born anew in each male human being. The little girl, with no powerful breasts, no penis, and no child, finds herself "organless" and therefore much more vulnerable to engulfment by the mother. The only opposition open to her is her ability to fantasize the powerful mother inside herself, and so she introjects her maternal imago and, within the psychic space carved for this internal object, she masters the omnipotent mother by freely directing both her libido and her aggression toward the internalized object. This internalized relationship with the mother is an attempt to substitute activity for passivity.

Unlike the boy, who can psychically almost totally obliterate the maternal imago, the girl introjects the mother, thereby controlling her. The libido expresses itself in the idea that "I am just like my mother," while the aggression fuels the Oedipal idea, "I will replace my mother and have Father's penis for myself." Aggression toward this internalized mother drives a girl's Oedipal conflict as much as love for the world and self-assertion or a sexual desire for the father; and in her unconscious fantasies, the little girl wins the love of her father by attacking her maternal introject. Herein lie the seeds of masochism.

Though the little girl actively attacks the mother in her attempt to steal the father from her, she cannot approach the father actively. She has no penis and comes to the father with the wish to receive something from him. She is compelled to identify with mother and take the passive position in terms of father. This sets up a split in the introjected maternal imago. The original, omnipotent, phallic mother of the life-giving breasts is associated with the mother–child dyad, not the male–female relationship. The little girl, if she wants to win father, must now modify the maternal imago and try to identify with the passive, submissive, "feminine" mother that is father's sexual partner. It is here that the concept of "penis" and "child" get merged in the female unconscious. Having a child would give the girl the power of the phallic mother, while having the penis would gain her access to the power of father. Father has both the penis and the power to give her a child, as he gave mother, so the female child turns to him with the hope of receiving access to both masculine and feminine power.

Sad to say, this situation is doomed from the beginning, for many reasons. The little girl perceives that her genital is much too small for her father's penis, and she fears she may be destroyed by it (Horney 1967). This creates anxiety not unlike the boy's fear of castration by his father if he has intercourse with his mother. The father for his part, if he is a good-enough father, is in no position to grant his daughter either his penis or a child. The cultural imposition of the incest barrier has hopefully restrained him in his impulse to have sex with and impregnate his daughter. But it is here that culture effects a more insidious prohibition. The father is a product of his own Oedipal travails, and very likely he has gained his masculine identity by devaluing and denying any dependence on females or any feminine identification within himself. He cannot perceive his daughter in the way he perceives his son, as an independent and autonomous subject.

Between father and daughter, there can be no mutual recognition (Benjamin 1988). He can only love her as an adored object. Whereas the father permits the son to identify with him, he unconsciously denies this tribute to his daughter. He rejects not only her desire for his manifest penis but also her wish for the idealized phallus as symbol of freedom from the engulfing mother. In so doing, he sets up a barrier to access to both the power of the female and the male. But his love for his daughter, so resonant of his love for her mother, tinged as it is with burgeoning sexuality, sends the unconscious message to her: "You will never possess a penis of your own, but you may someday receive a penis and a child, like your mother, provided you adopt the stance she has taken toward me."

Where does this leave the little girl? Her father's rejection of her certainly induces primitive aggression toward him, but if she expresses it directly, she risks loss of the hope of ever obtaining either the promised penis or child. If she turns the aggression back on her mother, she threatens the basis of her feminine identity and her only hope for ever gaining the power of the penis and child. The aggression must be both muted and redirected toward the self, and her destiny becomes to wait to receive. She must learn to enjoy being passive; barred access to actively loving, she must eroticize being loved. It is not, as Freud contended, that women need to be loved more than they can love. They are given no choice. They can neither suckle their mothers nor penetrate their fathers; their active loving has no external port and must, like their aggression, be turned back on the self. In this, they are aided by the love and tender feelings of mother and father and by culture, which has trained both parents to be more overtly affectionate with little girls than little boys and to permit much less direct expression of sexuality and aggression in their daughters than in their sons. The redirection of libido frustrated in its active outer aim, along with the internalization of tender parental feelings, infuse the female ego with the healthy narcissism that Deutsch equated with femininity. Because she has no penis, breasts, or child in her womb to focus this self-love upon, the girl tends to cathect the self more globally. Not only her entire body but also the products of her mind—her thoughts and feelings—become eroticized, giving the feminine personality its sensuality and emotional richness.

The phallic pre-Oedipal mother has a short-lived existence as a construct in the psyche of both sexes. Boys, armed as they are with the penis that opposes maternal omnipotence, obliterate this primitive pre-identification with the mother of the good and bad breast very early. And though girls avoid this act of psychic matricide, they lose their access to the powerful early mother for very different reasons, which have to do with the psychological wounds and stresses of the female Oedipal complex.

The infusion of secondary narcissism that Deutsch described in little girls is vital to female development because the reality of the female post-Oedipal position is harsh. The fact that female children adjust to that reality at all is a tribute to the enterprise of the feminine psyche—but the adaptation the little girl makes at this period is a shaky compromise at best.

Left empty and depressed by her father's rejection of both her sexual and identificatory love (Benjamin 1988) at the end of the Oedipal period, the girl experiences a kind of mourning. Turning back onto the primitive mother imago within, the girl regresses to her earlier oral mode of identification and this time incorporates her idealized, phallic father. This introjection of the powerful father achieves the same thing that the earlier maternal introjection accomplished—control over an essentially uncontrollable object—but it is not quite the same. When the female infant incorporated the phallic mother, it was a very primitive oral type of pre-identification, focused on bodily boundaries and the frontier between "inside" and "outside," a fantasy of ingesting the pre-Oedipal mother with her milk. The internalization of the Oedipal father is an introjection more than an incorporation. That is to say, it is a more highly evolved pre-identification because what is internalized is not only a mental representation of the object itself but also the inherent qualities of and the conflictual relationship to that object. The more mature and reality-oriented female child of the post-Oedipal period internalizes not only the imago of the father but also his feelings and behaviors. Since it is very likely that the father, because of the difficulties of becoming masculine in this world, has an unconscious or conscious tendency to defensively devalue women, this devaluation is internalized within the female psyche. So now the inner world consists of the residue and the mental image of the phallic mother, and also that of a real or fantasized relationship between maternal and paternal imagoes and between self and those imagoes. Within the ever-expanding inner space of her complex endopsychic world, the girl is free to discharge love and hate toward her internalized objects.

The internal triangle of maternal imago, paternal imago, and self is unique to female development. Boys reject their maternal introject to identify with their fathers, and this sets up a dualism of the male self as subject and the female other as object in the masculine unconscious. In the female psyche, this clear opposition doesn't exist. To some extent, all three elements of the girl's inner world are subjects. The girl's internalization of both mother and father allows her access to both her powerful, omnipotent mother and her potent, phallic father. This dual introjection is implicated in the bisexuality that Bonaparte and Chodorow asserted was characteristic of femininity. It is also responsible for women's unique way of looking at the world and framing morality. Freud's contention that the female superego is weaker than the male is perhaps too simplistic. The masculine superego is inexorable, impersonal, and independent of emotion because the boy has made a total identification with his powerful, phallic father and obliterated his primitive identification with his mother. This enables him to think in dualistic terms about right and wrong, good and bad. What Freud described as a weak superego is actually a uniquely feminine morality based on the complexity of the inner world. Since females have a triadic unconscious cathexis, they don't see morality in terms of rules and logic. Any ethical issue must be weighed from a variety of perspectives, and thus, is never resolved easily (Gilligan 1982).

Though the female triadic intrapsychic constellation provides women with an enormous capacity for identification, a rich inner life of imagination, fantasy, and intuition, and an ability to sacrifice self for others, these feminine virtues come at a high psychic price. Parental introjection presents a solution to the unique problems of the female Oedipal complex, but it also sets up new conflicts in the little girl's psyche. The shifting relationships and cathexis between the three points of the internal triangle have a profound effect on female psychic functioning, and the multitude of possibilities that exist between the three psychic structures allow for infinite individuality in female human beings.

There are trends in the triangular relationship, however, which offer explanation for several characteristics associated with femininity. First, the triangle is not equilateral. Both the introjected mother, with the child that father gave her and the breasts to feed it, and the introjected father, with his powerful penis, have endowments that the little girl does not possess. The self is compelled to take a subordinate position in relation to these powerful introjects, and this intrapsychic process conditions females to submission, self-abnegation, and passivity, to what Dinnerstein described as "the truly feminine woman's monstrously over-developed talent for unreciprocated empathy" (Dinnerstein 1976, 236). Even more damaging for feminine development than this subjugation of self to introjects is the intrapsychic relation between the maternal and paternal internalized objects. The maternal imago, initially a primary identification with the omnipotent and phallic mother of the oral period, has her omnipotence challenged when primary penis envy is established, but it is the introduction of the paternal imago at the resolution of the Oedipal conflict that has the most detrimental influence on the "mother-in-me." When the girl introjects her Oedipal father, she identifies with his wish to dominate and attack the maternal imago. She derives pleasure from neutralizing the omnipotence of the internalized mother—but this assault on her primary female identification provides fertile ground for the masochism and submission associated with femininity. Her identification and cooperation with dominating man gains her vicarious power, but at the price of devaluing her female identification. The muting of the drives, which Bonaparte described, probably is a defense against this toxic internal discord.

Latency brings about a repression of the conflict and initiates a period in which little girls pursue the acquisition of culture. The primary defenses of latency are projection and identification with the aggressor (Becker 1974). These defenses enable the girl to project masochistic tendencies onto her mother and identify with her father; thus, feminine eroticism and sensuality is temporarily abandoned for a more masculine focus on the outer world and education. Ironically, this active pursuit of what Edith Jacobson called a *Weltanschauung*, or "view of the world" (Jacobson 1961, 174), provides an initiation to patriarchal culture which can have a depressive effect on the pre-adolescent girl. Coming "up against the wall of Western culture," girls are in danger of losing their "voice" in their attempts to become feminine in a sexist society (Gilligan et al. 1989, 4). Gilligan's work seems to indicate that girls in early adolescence long to return to identification with a phallic mother. The conflict for Gilligan's research subjects is around finding a way to be both feminine and powerful. The problem for girls is that access to the primitive, powerful maternal introject of the first years of life is denied to them following the vicissitudes of the female Oedipal conflict. The intrapsychic conflict between the maternal and paternal internalized objects has demanded that female identification entail submission and passivity. Mother submits to father and self submits to both in this internalized relationship. Vacillating between the maternal and paternal introjects, girls struggle to define and strengthen the self in the psychic triangle. Helene Deutsch discussed the bisexual nature of the pre-pubertal period in girls. The girl wavers between the internalized mother and father and wants to have them both (Deutsch 1944).

With the strengthening of the sexual instincts at puberty, the libido toward internalized objects is intensified. But attachment to mother represents a greater danger than attachment to father. Libido directed toward the internalized maternal imago threatens a regression to the pre-Oedipal danger of engulfment by a phallic mother. Peter Blos wrote about the decisive and forceful turn toward heterosexuality that girls make to defend themselves against the phallic pregenital mother (Blos 1958). Identification with the father imago is heightened and revives the attack on the introjected mother. This two-sided discharge of aggression toward the mother creates a sense of guilt that is often expressed as attachments to same-sex friends and also provides impetus for the separation from primitive identifications which is adolescence's primary task. The girl's "best friend," whom she loves and with whom she shares everything, permits her to continue the experience of merging while denying feelings of narcissistic oneness with her mother (Chodorow 1978).

Recent writers have disputed the classic analytic theory that the work of adolescence is to separate from mother and father and asserted that the task is to find a way to stay connected while differentiating from parental figures (Gilligan et al. 1989). This debate can be resolved, however, when we make a clear differentiation between internal imagoes and actual objects. It is not mother and father that the female adolescent must relinquish; it is her primitive introjects of them. In actuality, the psychic work of feminine adolescence finally allows the young woman to see her parents realistically with all the hope for true intimacy that that implies. Hyman Spotnitz discussed the adolescent's typical obsession with "memory romances," fantasies pertaining to the romances of the Oedipal period. In the "winter of childhood," the young girl turns inward to her childhood objects, an attempt to understand backward in response to the anxieties involved in living forward (Spotnitz 1964, 223).

Peter Blos challenged the analytic view that the Oedipal complex is completely resolved at the end of the Oedipal period. Like Chodorow, Blos asserted that the resolution is only a partial one and that the Oedipal conflicts are not so much revived in adolescence as continued. The negative complex is particularly strong for adolescents and often manifests itself in intense hostility toward the parent of the same sex and a defensive clinging to the heterosexual component of the complex. Blos emphasized that the adolescent object disengagement through individuation proceeds in terms of internal, not external objects. Infantile parental imagoes perpetuate a belief in perfection, and separation implies a critical de-idealization and humanization of the infantile inner world. The great maturational surge in cognitive functioning at puberty permits the formation of a girl's own view of the past, present, and future, with the past being subjected for the first time to a kind of reality testing. Residual historical traumas must be integrated into the personality, where they provide organizers that promote the consolidation of the adult personality and account for its uniqueness. All elements of the internalized triangle must be de-idealized and replaced by the mature ambivalence that permits a turn to the object world and an adult sexualized relationship (Blos 1976).

In this difficult task of de-idealization and reconfiguration of her inner world, the adolescent girl is aided by the infusion of narcissism that Deutsch felt was so helpful. In the psychic triadic constellation of the pre-adolescent girl, the self has been compelled to take a subordinate position to the parental imagoes. With the surge of narcissism typical of this period, the "I am I" is born (Deutsch 1944, 95). This "I" is carved out of an intense internal struggle, characterized by what Deutsch described as the "clash between progressive and regressive forces" in which the young woman vacillates between a wish to return to symbiotic oneness with a phallic mother and a desire to kill her off and identify with the phallic father (Deutsch 1944, 115).

The onset of the menses is a profound psychic event in the life of a young girl. Deutsch said that menstruation "mobilizes psychic reactions so numerous and varied that we are justified in speaking of the "psychology of menstruation" (Deutsch 1944, 149). The first menstruation is usually experienced as a trauma. Deutsch related it to both the female castration complex and the reproductive function. The menses revives powerful feelings toward the mother, inspiring aggressive as well as sexual tendencies. Bleeding is associated in the unconscious with the old fantasy of castration, and the blame for that castration clearly belongs on mother's shoulders. The adolescent girl, like mother, is unclean and shameful; they share "secrets." There is also intense erotic pleasure at the thought of these "secrets." At last, she is initiated into that society of females to which she was denied access so long ago. The onset of menstruation comes with the promise that one day she will share in the power of the phallic mother. Sexual instincts are reawakened from regression and the girl takes her own body as an object of self-love and nurturance. Narcissistic vulnerability, particularly focused on the genitals, is expressed in the rejection of anything that might destroy their integrity. The vagina is alternately seen as something dirty and something very valuable (Deutsch 1944). Unless penis envy, in any of its forms, is too intense, menstruation initiates a turn toward an identification with the mother, but again, this is not the phallic mother of the pre-Oedipal period. Now the identification is with a more passive, truly "feminine" mother, the "wounded" mother who bleeds. This shift in the maternal imago is fueled by aggression expressed in the idea that mother and I are dirty and debased, but it also has a libidinal component. Now the girl has a valuable "jewel," and like mother, she can use her femininity to get the baby and the penis from father. Because of this altered feminine identification, the sexual instinct becomes infused with feeling and spirituality, giving female sexuality its unique eroticism.

Menstruation can also alter the female self's attitude toward the paternal introject. Deutsch reported that the unconscious idea of the young woman seems to be, "You didn't protect me from her" (Deutsch 1944, 121). The menses is manifest evidence that identification with the phallic father is hopeless. The unconscious anger aroused by this final negation of identificatory love along with the surge of sexuality that menstruation initiates create a strong tendency in young women to turn away from their fathers toward heterosexuality in the object world. Originally, this love may be idealized and focused on an admired teacher or a famous film star, but eventually heterosexual object choices will be more realistic, with attraction containing unconscious residues of both maternal and paternal imagoes (Klein 1964).

The sexual impulses directed toward the internal father are redirected out into the object world, while sexual impulses toward the maternal imago express themselves in the wish for a child, which is the desire to return to narcissistic oneness with the primitive mother.

The adolescent girl must now deal with a conflict or a harmony of many contradictory elements. Questions of masculine versus feminine, active versus passive, and autonomy versus connection will challenge her sense of self. These questions become associated in her mind with the internalized parental objects along sexual lines. Much more than boys, girls incorporate traits associated with the opposite-sex parent into their identities, though often after the trauma of the first menses and the identification with the wounded mother, these "masculine" qualities are experienced as unattainable ideals rather than integrated character traits. The internal maternal and paternal imagoes are seldom in harmony at this point in development; though the phallic father rarely supersedes and deposes the passive mother, it is just as rare that the struggle between them ends in a tie.

The intrapsychic problem for young women is that many of the qualities they most desire—active sexuality, autonomy, assertiveness, power—are the provenance of the father within and, as such, threaten their female identification. The internal triangle lacks what Jessica Benjamin called *intersubjectivity*, a situation where two subjects, different but equal, confront each other's differences in mutual recognition (1988). The intrapsychic relationship between father and mother is one between subject and object; and though adolescence is characterized by the ascendance of the self in terms of introjected objects, the paternal imago can dominate the internal triangle in a way that makes adjustment to femininity challenging. The healthy tension between self-assertion and recognition of and connection to the other is often not attained in adolescence. Young women often split their identifications along gender lines and become passive and depressed if they cathect the wounded mother, or ambitious and aggressive if identified with their phallic father imago. True integration of the complex female inner world is a task that continues for life.

CHAPTER TWO

The Object Within: Childbirth as a Developmental Milestone

Childbirth is a developmental milestone in feminine life, as psychically significant for women as the Oedipus complex and adolescence. It provides opportunities for maturation and psychic reconstruction and reconfiguration unique in the life cycle. My two-year work with two groups of pregnant women confirmed that female development is not something that ends when adolescence is over. Rather, feminine developmental issues continue to be reworked in conflict and resolution throughout a woman's life. Dynamics derived from the pre-Oedipal and Oedipal periods are not abolished or abandoned. They are built upon and integrated into the personality in compromises of ever-expanding complexity.

Bibring (1961) defined a developmental phase as a turning point in the life cycle leading to intense disequilibrium, which results, in favorable circumstances, in specific maturational steps toward new functions. Given this definition, pregnancy and childbirth qualify as a legitimate developmental phase. Like adolescence and menopause, pregnancy is a crisis which creates profound life changes with which women must deal. Pregnancy demands a reworking of the relationship to one's internalized parental objects, particularly the resolution of the infantile aspects of those relationships. Bibring described the specific task of childbirth as the redistribution of the cathexis of self-representations and of object representations. A specific sequence and alteration of the woman's object libidinal and narcissistic positions occurs in pregnancy (Bibring 1961). This chapter will detail exactly how these new psychic constructs occur.

Helene Deutsch called pregnancy a "kind of late maturation" (Deutsch 1945, 56). It is helpful to female growth and functioning because it tends to thrust a woman's inner world into the object field where it can be dealt with in terms of reality. Of course, this maturation can be achieved in other ways, but pregnancy and childbirth—because they are rooted in the body and often cause women to regress to their own pre-Oedipal, indeed their intrauterine, life—provide powerful primitive fuel for unconscious change.

Several themes emerged about pregnancy and childbirth in my work with women. The first and most apparent is an idea that Freud (1931) first discussed: pregnancy forces women to confront their own mothers. In the unconscious, getting pregnant means "becoming my mother." The simple statement, "I'll afraid I'll turn into my mother," was virtually a universal idea in the minds of women contemplating childbirth and I began to see that it reflected both a fear and a wish. Women who absolutely refused the notion of "becoming mother" were the ones who decided not to have babies or were infertile, despite their conscious wishes to have children (Spotnitz, Freeman, 1969). A childless woman who had been raised in an orphanage said, "I have no mother. I don't know how to mother." Another infertile woman, who had had no contact with her mother for two years, remarked, "My mother just has to realize that I am not her, and she is not me." Sometimes this rejection of maternal identification was instigated by the woman's mother. A fifty-three-year-old childless woman told me:

> I think on some level, my mother didn't want me to be a mother. She was the only one who was allowed to be a mother, so I had to be something else. She told me once that she thought she had never really given birth to me, never really let me be born. She hadn't let me separate from her. When I look back on my life, I always said I wanted children, but I didn't act like I did. I think I made the decisions I made because I didn't want to turn into my mother, and the only way not to turn into my mother was not to mother.

Women who were able to forgive and accept their mothers seemed to more readily accept the mothering role themselves. Annette told us about her own mother who hadn't protected her against sexual abuse from her stepfather, "My mother did wrong to me, but I forgave her because I loved her. She should have protected me, but she was afraid. When she got cancer, I nursed her until she died. She was vomiting blood, but I rocked her like a baby." Annette, pregnant for the second time, wanted to study social work because "I like to help people. I like to take care of them." She was fiercely protective of her own child: "My mother never protected me, but I carried my girl around on my back." She seemed to be saying, "I am a better mother than my mother was." She gained power over her maternal introject with her own motherly stance.

Pregnancy reactivates a longing to be mothered and the wish to be a baby. Regressing to orality, women in both groups talked endlessly about chocolate milk and fried foods. Dreams reported by the women were often set in their "mother's houses," a symbol of the womb, expressing the wish to return to the pre-Oedipal and even prenatal symbiosis. One pregnant woman reported the following dream, "I dreamed I saw this big, beautiful house, and I thought, 'It's so nice. My mother and I can live there.' But then my mother fell down the stairs and got killed." The wish to be symbiotic and the idea that birth (falling down the stairs) ends that symbiosis and obliterates union with mother were apparent in the dream. One of the most frightening things about pregnancy for many women is the regression to prenatal and pre-Oedipal periods that it involves. Naomi said, "I feel like I'm losing myself to my body." Another patient complained, "I cry all the time, and when I look in the mirror, I look just like a weeping infant, a big baby." This regression often involves the danger that the woman will be engulfed by her pre-Oedipal mother, and fear of this danger plays a part in many cases of infertility (Davis 1985).

The idea that pregnancy implies a return to issues of symbiosis, while childbirth seems to permit the termination of that symbiosis with the woman's own mother, is illustrative of a paradox in pregnancy: It requires an identification with mother for the unconscious to permit pregnancy, but by identifying with mother enough to get pregnant, a woman can finally, in childbirth, achieve true individuation and psychic separation from mother. More specifically, women can achieve pregnancy only by having a certain unconscious willingness to confront the maternal introject. The maternal introject in women is a synthesis of two imagoes: the pre-Oedipal mother and the passive, "feminine" mother who is the inheritor of the Oedipus complex. It is important to remember that, for both sexes, the pre-Oedipal mother is not "castrated." Rather she is a primal, omnipotent figure. Her breasts, the part-objects that introduce the baby to the world, are protruding organs of activity and penetration, the source of life. Crowell discussed the toxic aspects of both the powerful mother introject and the depressed, passive, feminine image of mother (Crowell 1981).

Fears of regressing and becoming the phallic pre-Oedipal mother's helpless infant—as well as anxieties about becoming the passive, masochistic mother of the Oedipus complex—play a significant part in both infertility and early pregnancy. By identifying with the "feminine" mother and submitting passively and masochistically to pregnancy, women overcome those fears and truly identify, for the first time in the life cycle, with the powerful pre-Oedipal maternal imago, thus achieving individuation and autonomy while integrating a feminine identification. The process of gestating the fetus and pushing it out into the world permits the ego a new stance toward the maternal internalized object. Childbirth seems to facilitate true identification with the phallic mother of the pre-Oedipal period, so that the self is no longer controlled or dominated by its maternal imago. Pregnancy allows separation from the engulfing mother in a uniquely feminine way. In childbirth, the woman gains the power her mother had in the pre-Oedipal period and, by total identification with that power, women reconcile autonomy and femininity. They can at last identify with their mothers without submitting to engulfment. A patient who had recently had a baby, and whose mother was staying with her to help her take care of the newborn, made the following observation:

> I was changing the baby, and my mother was watching, and I said, "Here, Mom, take her while I throw this diaper away." And I gave the baby to my mother, and she took the baby, and she was very nervous, and I had a revelation while I watched my mother hold my daughter. My mother was *scared*, and she felt inadequate, and she was afraid she was going to hurt the baby. And then, I saw that she got angry at the baby for giving her all those awful feelings, and just then, the baby started to cry, and in that moment, I understood everything about my own character and how it was formed, all the sadness and guilt and shame that's a part of me. I've hated my mother, but in that little moment, I realized she couldn't help it. She did the best she could. I identified with my mother and my daughter both. I understood exactly how my daughter felt, and for the first time, I understood my mother too. I didn't know which one of them to hold. But I put my arms around my mother. I loved them both, and I loved me too. And for the first time, I felt in control of my life. Because I understood everything.

This patient applied the role of phallic mother to both her own mother and herself in relation to her new baby. She got "control of my life" by simultaneously identifying with fetus/self and self/mother, and viewing the pre-Oedipal scene with a healthy observing ego that was powerful, because she "understood everything." This opportunity to perceive the pre-Oedipal situation as an adult observer, while identifying with all the characters in that situation, is one of the beneficial aspects of childbearing. It allows for an unconscious integration of the complex endopsychic world.

The Paternal Image

This integration is characterized by a strengthening of ego in relation not only to the internalized mother but also to the paternal introject. Another paradox of pregnancy concerns the internalized father. Pregnancy, or even the thought of pregnancy, tends to heighten aggression toward men in a woman's mind (Spotnitz and Freeman 1969). This aggression directed toward males was particularly strong in the group I ran for disadvantaged women. Men were "mama's boys" who acted like "big babies." One woman said, "Sometimes I wonder who's pregnant, him or me? All he does is lie around, sleeping and eating and expecting to be waited on." Another told her boyfriend, "Any idiot can make a baby, but it takes a man to be a father." When he hit her in response, she said, "'You're never going to see this baby. If something is trash, you put it in the garbage.' I sent him back to his mother." Annette reported, "Since I been pregnant, I been having the scariest dreams. They're all about killing. They're all about killing little boys. Once I dreamed I was killing a baby, and a little boy was helping me." Later, Annette had another dream about killing a male: "I dreamed I had an abortion, but the baby came out, and it was talking to me. It was a little boy baby, and it started talking to me. It was horrible." Almost every woman in the group said from time to time, "I don't need no man in my life. I got my baby, and that's all I need." A woman who arrived with her week-old infant said about the father of her child, "I don't want no part of him. I don't need him around. I'll be fine by myself. I can take care of my own." There was a sense that, now that the women had their fetus/baby, they didn't need a penis. But there was also a wish to be babied by their men and rage at the men for not being willing to be mothering to them. As one patient said, "When a man gets a woman pregnant, it's his responsibility to provide for her. He has to make a home for her and take care of her and the baby. But these men are such children. They can make these babies all right, but then they go back to their mothers and act like big babies themselves." Primitive competitive triangles between a pregnant woman, the father of her child, and his mother were commonly reported, and these conflicts always struck me as being more about who would be allowed to be babied than about Oedipal, sexual rivalry.

In my other group, there was talk of men abandoning women in pregnancy. The women weren't sure their partners would protect and support them. A patient had the following dream:

> I was nine months pregnant, and I started to hemorrhage. There was all this blood, and I was so scared. I was in my mother's house, the house I grew up in,

> and she was screaming at me. Somehow it was my husband's fault that we were there. I don't know how it worked, but somehow, he was allowing it. He was there, and he wasn't protecting me against my mother. He was accommodating her. We were trying to go to the hospital, and my mother wanted to go with us, and I didn't want that, and my husband was siding with her.

This dream, both a fear and a wish, seems to say that the husband was putting her at risk by getting her pregnant, which meant abandoning her to the engulfing pre-Oedipal mother. Another woman resisted pregnancy because her husband would work fourteen-hour days and render her a victim of their baby: "I'll be alone and in a panic, just like my mother was." Many women reported anxieties about their husbands leaving them. I often surmised that all of the fear of being abandoned by men was actually an unconscious wish to get rid of them. Several women were able to use their pregnancies to forge new relationships with their actual fathers and their paternal imagoes. Lily, who had always handled her father with a defensive and distant friendliness, reported "finally telling him off" after her baby was born. A woman in the group who had given birth a few weeks before reported, "I finally let my father have it after all those years of being silently offended." Another patient spoke of "feeling more like my father's mother than his daughter" after she gave birth.

Many of the pregnant women in both groups verbalized the idea when pregnant that they were not going to be dominated by men anymore. Lily called it "training" her husband, while Martha called it "threatening." The women in the disadvantaged group said over and over that at about eight months into the pregnancy, their men, who had been acting like big babies and withdrawing from them throughout most of their pregnancies, wanted to be "under" them again. But the women held back: "Let him see how it feels."

After their babies were born, several of the group members related interesting stories about their new babies and their own fathers. I heard often of the importance of presenting the newborn to the father. One woman said:

> When I got home from the hospital, my mother and father came over, and I felt so glad to see them. I felt really close to my mother, but it's funny, when they came in, I right away gave the baby to my father. For some reason, it was very important for him to hold the baby. I just wanted to present him with his grandson.

Another patient with a male analyst told a remarkably similar story:

> I took the baby to my first analytic session after we came home from the hospital. I had had this fantasy for days that I wanted my analyst to hold the baby.

> Just hold it. I don't know why. When I arrived, I asked him if he would mind holding the baby just for a moment before I lay down on the couch. He was initially reluctant and I could see he was uncomfortable. But I said, "Please, just for a moment. It's very important to me." He took the baby, and she looked up at him, and he was silent for a moment, and then he said, "Oh my, this is a very special baby." I felt euphoric.

Langer (1992) talked about the fetus as something "stolen" from the mother. These vignettes seem to confirm this idea. Women seemed to act out the idea that their babies were fathered, not by their husbands, but by their fathers or their father representatives. Childbirth had, on an unconscious level, finally made them Oedipal winners with the childish fantasy of obtaining a penis/child from their father at last fulfilled.

This data lent credence to the theory that pregnancy initially heightens aggression toward the internalized father, then finally achieves a restructuring of the relationship between the ego and the paternal imago, with the self acquiring a new authority in terms of the paternal introject. Childbirth seems to help a woman experience herself as what Benjamin (1988, 12) called a "sovereign equal" to a man—and not by a defensive imitation of masculine power, but by an identification with a truly female power. The internal relationship shifts from one between a subject/father and object/self and becomes a more integrated interplay between subject and subject. The new relationship between ego and paternal imago is what Benjamin called "a dance of mutual recognition" (130). In some cases, women actually seemed to use their pregnancies to replace their mothers on the level of fantasy and shift the internal relationship from one between father/female-child to father/mother.

One reason that pregnancy and childbirth can give a woman this new sense of power is that, in many ways, pregnancy functions for women as a penis does for men. Simone de Beauvoir (1952) wrote eloquently about how the penis operates for men. She felt that the major benefit of the penis is that by a boy's having an organ that can be seen and grasped, he can partially identify himself with it: "He projects the mystery of his body, its threats, outside himself, which enables him to keep them at a distance. Because he has an alter ego, in whom he sees himself, the little boy can boldly assume an attitude of subjectivity; the very object on which he projects himself becomes a symbol of autonomy, of transcendence, of power" (278). De Beauvoir talked about the double role the penis plays:

> It is for him at once a foreign object and himself. It becomes an alter ego, ordinarily more artful, more intelligent, and more clever than the individual.

> The penis is regarded by the subject as at once himself, and other than himself; its functions are midway between the voluntary and the involuntary, and because it is capricious and, as it were, a foreign source of pleasure that is felt subjectively. The individual's specific transcendence takes concrete form in the penis, and it is a source of pride. The phallus assumes such worth as it does because it symbolizes dominance that is exercised in other domains. If woman should succeed in establishing herself as a subject, she would invent equivalents of the phallus. (de Beauvoir 1952, 278)

I suggest that pregnancy and childbirth function as equivalents of the phallus. Like the penis, the fetus is self and non-self, both subject and object; this double role gives woman the self-containment and self-reliance that the penis gives man. Like the penis, the pregnancy compensates for early narcissistic wounds, the old trauma of feeling "organless." Like the penis, the pregnancy and the fetus represent bodily symbols of independence from the engulfing pre-Oedipal mother. The newborn, like the phallus, can be seen and grasped and partially identified with. A new mother can see the self/object that is her child and know that the child can function. A woman's internal conflicts and anxieties can be projected onto the fetus and kept at a distance, providing the same function that de Beauvoir described in terms of the penis. The baby/fetus is its mother phallic alter ego, an object over which the mother can assume an attitude of subjectivity and yet at the same time, feel that object to be a part of the self. In giving birth, a woman achieves what little boys achieved with the castration complex: detachment and autonomy from the maternal imago. Just as the penis allows men to see themselves as totally separate and independent from women, so does the protruding belly of pregnancy give women that independence from the maternal imago.

If the fetus can be seen as equivalent to the penis as a dynamic in psychic functioning, it is significant that women must give up the valued self-object in a way that men never have to. Castration fantasies are crucial to male development, but they remain fantasies; men are never required to relinquish their penises as women must lose the pregnancy and the fetus in childbirth. The loss of the phallus/fetus means that women must perceive the self/object as a separate object, and this is a process which is painful and by no means ever completely accomplished. Chodorow effectively described the boundary confusion and lack of individuation so common in women (Chodorow 1978). But the projection of the self/object into the outer world, as traumatic as it is, can have positive psychic consequences. It can act as an impetus to individuation and a remedy against narcissism. In *Psychoanalysis and Feminism*, Juliet Mitchell discussed the path out of primitive narcissism:

> The object is first realized as an object in its absence. Both the recognition of the separateness of the object and (it is the same thing) of the self can, then, only come through a knowledge of absence. For One to exist at all, two are needed, even if the second is in fact the reflection in the mirror. Because he stayed hooked on his own image and couldn't tolerate its absence, Narcissus never constituted himself as subject. The very self, the subject, is only created in difference. The illusion of primordial unity is Zero that misthinks itself as One. (Mitchell 1974, 383)

The dual whole of man/penis or woman/fetus can be experienced as narcissistic bliss, but for women that bliss is shattered by labor and delivery. And though the termination of that bliss is painful, it also provides a pathway out of narcissism, the inability to recognize the other as a separate object. The ability to see another who, until moments ago, was a part of self makes it impossible to narcissistically deny recognition of the object world of separately sentient others, and equally impossible not to identify with those others on some level. The loss of self/object then, with its demand that the object be realized as both like the self and different from it, becomes a maturational leap for a woman. Childbirth helps women achieve what Jessica Benjamin called *intersubjectivity*, where sameness and difference between two subjects (not a subject and an object) exist in the healthy tension of mutual recognition (Benjamin 1988). So the loss of the child/penis can be a developmental milestone, albeit an agonizing one, which can be experienced as traumatic as death.

Childbirth is certainly linked with death in the unconscious. The loss of the self/object in childbirth is one reason for this link. Another is the primitive regression to symbiotic union and the loss of that symbiosis that are associated with death that childbirth symbolizes.

Over and over, my clients talked about childbirth in ways that brought death to mind. They were "losing control." They had "to go through this alone." They talked of "going someplace I've never gone before." Everything was going to change. There was tremendous fear of the "unknown": "I just can't imagine how it will be." Lisa talked incessantly about her fear of the pain of birth and she insisted, "I have to go through it alone. I don't want nobody to see me suffer or scream. I'm scared, I'm scared, but it's just something I have get through." She could have been talking about birth or death, and her remarks demonstrated the link between them. When the first pregnant woman in my group actually gave birth, the group didn't meet for several weeks. Everyone called in sick or didn't show up. It was like, with the actual birth of a child, the group had become a place as frightening as death.

Because the baby is both self and object, childbirth is a loss of both, a kind of death, and postpartum grief and mourning that is experienced as depression is common in women. The loss of self/object that pushing a baby into the world implies was eloquently described by a patient who talked about the hours after the birth of her baby:

> I lay in bed weeping. I felt the loss of her so profoundly. I thought of all the people, long dead, who had helped me make her. My husband's father, I never knew him, but his blood is running though her veins. My grandmother, who died last year, and all the generations and generations of my family way back to Ireland, all dead, who helped me make her. I realized that now, just as the hour and day of her birth is determined, can be written down on a birth certificate, so the hour and day of her death will be written on a death certificate someday. As long as she was inside me, she was safe, immortal, a timeless fantasy. Now I have lost her to the world. She is flesh and blood, limited, manifest, and ultimately mortal.

It is the triumph of life over death that makes a successful childbirth experience empowering and ego-enhancing. Pregnancy is dangerous but it is in confronting that danger that women overcome entropy and become truly alive. Experiencing childbirth means feeling through in a primitive way what it is to be human, to be a part of an essentially uncontrollable process that started before we were born and will continue after we die. Pregnancy and childbirth as powerful life forces that can confront and triumph over the death instinct were ideas that were apparent in all the trauma, violence, and death that were part of the disadvantaged group. Despite all the abuse they endured, women said over and over, "I have to be strong for the baby." Everyone wanted to go back to school or give up drugs, since "it's not just me now." Indeed, pregnancy seemed to offer some protection against violence. One father who had picked up a pipe had second thoughts, "You know I can't hit you when you're pregnant." For all the women in both groups, pregnancy seemed to motivate them to stay connected to significant others and to move closer to objects who had been defensively pushed away.

Shifting Object Representations

One of the most interesting aspects of my research was the observation of shifting object representations in pregnancy. The fetus within is the receptacle for all sorts of fantasies and projections. It can alternately be perceived as the self or one of the internalized parental objects, as part of her body or the parasite that feeds on it, as the possessed or the possessor.

Rabuzzi (1994) described the infant within as the "motherself," a binary-unitary that is both two and one at the same time, with its parts consisting of mother and child in varying degrees of relationship. Poet Adrienne Rich (1976) put it this way:

> In pregnancy, I did not experience the embryo as decisively internal in Freud's terms, but rather as something inside and of me, yet becoming hourly and daily more separate on its way to becoming separate from me and of itself. In early pregnancy, the stirrings of the fetus felt like ghostly tremors of my own body, later like the movements of a being imprisoned in me; but both sensations were my sensations, contributing to my own sense of physical and psychic space. The child that I carry for nine months can be defined neither as me nor not-me. Far from existing in the mode of "inner space," women are powerfully and vulnerably attuned to both "inner" and "outer," because, for us, the two are continuous, not polar. (63)

The ambivalence and vacillation in her feelings and fantasies about her infant in a pregnant woman create all sorts of maternal attitude changes during the course of fetal development. The vomiting of early pregnancy can indicate a certain refusal of the pregnancy. One patient called the fetus a "tumor" when she was in the throes of morning sickness. Midway through pregnancy, the nausea usually abates, and many of my patients experienced a sense of peace and well-being. Though they were aware that the baby was there, mother and fetus often seemed in perfect attunement. This is how one patient put it:

> I loved the middle three months. For the first time in my life, I wasn't alone in my own skin. I felt "two in one." The pain of existential loneliness was gone, and I had no anxiety. I just felt like, "What could go wrong? We're together." The baby's movements were coordinated with mine and yet distinct. It was great. But then when the baby started getting so big, and its kicking really started to hurt, and I got indigestion and couldn't breathe, and felt a foot jammed against my ribs, I began to think, "Why don't you get the hell out of there, you little intruder? You're wearing out your welcome." And at the end, I was terribly anxious and conflicted. I wanted it to be over and at the same time, I was terrified of the labor and delivery. No way out.

This attunement followed by conflict between fetus and child was very common. When women approach delivery, all their primitive terrors come to life, and they fear they will die in birth. There is an acute conflict between retaining the precious fetus, which has been part of ego and yet also treasured object, and expelling the expanding invader. As the pregnancy unfolds, a woman must more and more separate the baby from her own ego and experience it as an object toward whom she feels both libido and aggression.

Psychoanalyst Alessandra Piontelli (1992) has, in recent years, used ultrasound technology to observe fetuses in utero. Piontelli's beautiful pictures of fetuses floating in the amniotic fluid make it clear that character exists in the womb. Particularly in observing twins, Piontelli was able to offer dramatic evidence that two fetuses growing in the same woman display totally different patterns of activity, in contact and withdrawal and in quantities of libido and aggression, and that these character patterns persist after birth. Piontelli's work seems to lend credence to the idea that many of a human being's most deep-seated characterological issues are representations of sensory perceptions experienced in utero and recorded in the primitive unconscious in a way that makes them a powerful dynamic in the formation of psyche. In pregnancy, a woman unconsciously projects some of these early pre-feelings, which she experienced in her own prenatal life, onto her fetus. This provides an opportunity in pregnancy to unconsciously work through deep-seated prenatal issues by utilizing the projections onto the child within. Furthermore, the physical act of pushing a baby into the world is a psychic and physical projection of the inner world to the outer world; this means that the pre-feeling conflicts invested in the fetus during pregnancy are pushed from fantasy to reality where they become available to be utilized and resolved by the mature observing ego of the new mother.

Baby as self can manifest itself as fetus as alien intruder, the woman's own voracious intrauterine and pre-Oedipal self who wished to eat her mother up and destroy her. Alternately, baby/self can represent an ego ideal; in this case, you observe that the pregnant woman is taking better care of herself, is more responsible, and has greater social consciousness, all for the sake of the beloved baby as idealized self. A pregnant woman I interviewed said:

> I grew up fast. Pregnancy had an immediate maturational effect on me. I used to have trouble doing the responsible thing. Like the amnio. In the past I would have been afraid it would hurt, and I would have just forgotten to do it. But now I thought, "No way am I going to forget this. This is important." It's not just me anymore.

The protective feelings that women verbalized and the common desire to talk to the unborn baby were examples of the fetus representing the infant/self, and the pregnant woman's wish to baby herself by babying her fetus. Even after the child is born, women experience the infant as an extension of self, and gratification of the child serves the same psychological purpose as gratification of the self. In nurturing their babies, women were identified with their own mothers and at the same time with their infants; in providing care, they re-experienced themselves as cared-for babies, thus sharing with their babies the possession of a good mother. Baby as self can also be associated with the idea of defective self. Dreams of giving birth to monsters and retarded infants were common in my groups and reflected the fantasy of baby as inadequate, pathological self.

The fetus can also be perceived as an object, and again these object representations can shift and reintegrate during pregnancy and birth. Baby as alien can also represent a toxic introject, either maternal or paternal. Aggression against these representations was rampant in all my work with women and manifested itself as compulsive worry about the baby and about harming the baby, which I interpreted as unconscious wishes to destroy the fetus. Dreams of killing babies were common. In both groups, women obsessed about hurting their infants by sleeping on their stomachs, drinking coffee, buying dangerous baby gear, and countless other creative ways to destroy the object within.

The process of analysis leads to the re-externalization of internalized or introjected objects, and the reworking through and re-internalization occurs in such a way that there is a radical change in mental structure (Loewald 1962). Pregnancy and childbirth, particularly when experienced in conjunction with psychoanalysis, seem to provide the same function. Just as psychoanalysis allows people to be "awake and aware" about their intrapsychic dynamics, in order to develop an observing ego that can modulate and regulate conflict, so do educated pregnancies and undrugged childbirths allow women to be present at the restructuring of their inner world that marks childbirth as a significant developmental milestone.

The interplay between internalization and externalization of introjected objects, along with the vacillating cathexes of the representation of the fetus as self and object make childbirth a time of heightened identifications for women. Masculine and feminine identifications, which have been in conflict in the endopsychic world of the internal triangle of maternal and paternal introjects and self, tend to become more integrated. Rather than a relationship of subject/object that has characterized the dynamic between paternal imago and maternal imago and between both parental imagoes and self, a restructuring occurs which allows for a triangle of equal subjects. Power, autonomy, individuation, "masculine" qualities, which heretofore have often been the sole property of the internalized father, become associated with the maternal imago and with the self, and not in a defensively "masculine" way, but in a manner endowed with a truly feminine strength, the strength of the pre-Oedipal mother. The integration of "masculine" and "feminine" that the following case of Naomi illustrates was by no means the exception. Many new mothers demonstrated this new complexity of identifications.

In addition, the demand that pregnancy and childbirth make that a woman perceive a part of her self as an object often sets up a heightened capacity to identify with the world and everyone in it. A patient described this dynamic:

> Since I got pregnant, I feel I have more empathy for people. I see how vulnerable everyone is, how pulled along by life. Maybe that's because I feel vulnerable and out of control, pushed along by the life force. But I just feel everyone's feelings. I feel connected to every other human being on a really deep level. I sense people's struggles, and I identify with them.

Another woman put it this way:

> After Emily was born, I just felt connected to everybody. I used to watch the news at night and see people dying in wars or starving in Ethiopia and feel indifferent, removed. Now I weep. It's as if it's happening to me now, to Emily. I want to get involved in helping people in some way.

The dual identification with "masculine" power and "feminine" connection that childbirth seems to help instigate achieves new levels of complexity and integration in the female psyche.

I would like to address the question of whether there is a true maternal instinct, an instinct toward reproduction in women. Freud believed this powerful wish was really a wish for a penis (Freud 1932). Karen Horney (1967) and other psychoanalytic theorists disagreed with Freud, believing that there is a biological instinct in women that compels them to have babies. Feminist writers have insisted that mothering is by no means innate; rather, it is learned, or that culture "brainwashes" women into having babies.

In working with women, I have come to believe that there is a powerful maternal instinct, one which has its origins in the intrauterine life of girls. I believe the maternal instinct is a repetition compulsion, a desire to return to oneness with the mother. Chodorow (1978) pointed out that all people who have been mothered have a wish to return to the exclusive symbiosis of the mother–child dyad. Men attempt to return to this unity in sexual intercourse, but this pathway is not open to women. By having a child, woman can resolve and recreate the mother–daughter bond. Only in pregnancy and childbirth can women re-experience the narcissistic oneness that preceded the first sensation. From this point of view, pregnancy and childbirth are a wish to return to a state of nontension, a death instinct in the service of life. It is this primitive integration of life and death that makes childbirth so awesome and so terrifying to every human being. And it is the triumph of libido over aggression that makes pregnancy so empowering. One of my patients talked about the "special club" that having a baby admits you to. No longer estranged from their bodies, women saw them as "the seat of magical powers." A new mother said, "I've changed. Now I know how things work. And now I know what I know." When the child leaves the body it leaves a residue behind, a sense that goodness and power are inside rather than outside the body, a talisman to carry for life.

The Case of Naomi

Naomi was three months pregnant when she came into treatment for anxiety. She said, "I'm afraid I'm going to turn into my mother and just give up my whole life to motherhood, like my mother did. One reason I think I got pregnant so easily is that I have a very good mother, but she totally sacrificed herself to motherhood. I don't want that." She was vomiting constantly. Naomi admitted her pregnancy was unplanned. "It wasn't my choice. I think I got pregnant because my husband wanted a baby so badly."

Naomi told me she came from a very close and traditional family. She said, "The women have the babies and raise them, and the men kill themselves with work. My father is so sexist. You can't believe how he talks to my mother, though she holds her own. He's very rigid too. He insisted I go to dancing lessons. I wanted to drive a truck, but he wouldn't let me. My mother is a wonderful mother, but she never worked. I'm a feminist, and my mother was a feminist too, but look at her now. I watched my mother have nothing to live for but the children. She was the nurturer. So that's how I learned to be a nurturer."

Naomi was a stockbroker, but "this baby has screwed up all my plans to develop my career. I worry about giving up my job, my whole life. I want to work." Her mother would be taking care of the baby after it was born. "I feel a little guilty about this," she said, "My mother has been taking care of kids all her life, and she loves to do it, but I think she deserves a rest at this point in her life. Also I worry that if my mother takes care of the baby, I mean, she's great, but I worry that we're both going to forget who the mother is." Naomi was just beginning her career and her husband, a health-care consultant, made much more money than she did. "I want my husband to cut his work week back from five days to three, so I can work too, but he says it's out of the question. But I'm so worried about my career. I don't want to be dependent on someone to put food on the table." She said, "I'm not feeling at all feminine or successful. I feel like a fat cow."

Naomi wore her red hair cropped very short, and she favored pants. "I would never wear a frilly skirt," she said,

> I associate it with no choices. I really had no choices as a girl. I remember once I had a boyfriend who was an electrician, and he was showing me how light switches work, and I thought, "No one ever showed me any of this." No one ever gave me the option to be an electrician. I wanted to be a fireman. I feel so out of control now, and I guess I am, but that's part of life, and at a certain point, you just have to let go. I've got to keep working. I'm so scared I'm going to end up like my mother, just staying at home and never working again. Sometimes I really wish I had one of those "career woman" type mothers who are very successful in business. Why did I even think I wanted to get pregnant? I think it's because of my upbringing. I watched my mother have nothing to live for but the children, so I didn't know what else to do with myself. But I always envied my father going out of the house to his job. He was the provider. I think I want to be a combination of my mother and my father.

Naomi's feminism seemed to be in constant conflict with her pregnancy. She said, "I think men are afraid to show their feminine side. Sexism is like racism. People say they hate minorities, and then they leave their babies with black people to raise. My husband wants no part of this baby. He won't go to the doctor with me. I'm having to drag him to the classes. And he absolutely refuses to cut back to three days a week."

The tendency to worry became more pronounced as Naomi's pregnancy progressed. "I worry all the time about eating the wrong things. I drank two Diet Cokes, and I feel so guilty." She worried about caffeine. "I can't drink coffee or wine, and I feel so deprived." She would reassure herself by saying, "My mother drank, and she smoked, and all ten of us are fine." She worried about sleeping in the wrong position and smothering the baby. She worried about gaining too much weight. She worried about Sudden Infant Death Syndrome. She worried because she didn't feel maternal and wasn't sure she would. She worried about disciplining the baby. "My father used to hit me hard, and I worry if I get mad, I'll start hitting. I get so mad at my husband that I feel like hitting him, but I never have. My father used to fly into rages, and now I fly into rages." Above all, Naomi worried about being inadequate in terms of pregnancy and childbirth.

> Everybody talks about how horrible the pain is, and I'm afraid. And lately I've started worrying again that the baby is not all right. Early in the pregnancy, I

> used to feel it was so creepy to have something growing inside me. Did you ever see the movie *Alien*, where all those creepy things were growing inside her? I used to feel so horrible thinking there was a little alien growing inside me. But then it went away.

When I asked Naomi what had made it go away, she said, "I had an amnio, and that helped a little. But the sonogram made it seem real to me. I saw his arms and legs moving around, and I thought, 'What could go wrong? He's perfect. He's fine.' I think that's when I settled down and stopped thinking of him as an alien. Now I'm worrying again."

Naomi had wanted a midwife and a birth center for her delivery, but her father had insisted that she go to the family doctor, even though he was known as "Mr. C-Section." Naomi was very worried she would have a C-section too, but opposing her father seemed out of the question. She spent a lot of time in session reassuring herself that episiotomies and C-sections were sometimes the best way to go. "I just worry that I'm going to get in there in labor and not be able to stand up for myself, and things will start happening to me."

Naomi and her husband bought a house in the suburbs. She was unhappy about the decision and hated the new house. I asked her why she would buy a house she hated. She said, "Because it was so important to my husband." The only thing Naomi liked about the move is that she would be right down the street from her mother. "I need to be close to my mother. I need her, but I feel so guilty about using her. She gave up her life for us."

As Naomi's due date approached, her anxiety increased. She said,

> I think when I start my contractions, I'll go right to my mother's house. I just want to go right up to my old room and lock the door. I don't want my mother with me. I'd just like to have my husband and me alone together in my old room when I have the baby. I can't believe my due date is so close. I guess it's never seemed real to me. Now I realize, I'm really going to have a baby. I know he's real. I feel him move. He kicks me in the ribs, and it really hurts, so I've always been aware that inside me is another human being.

I asked her if she liked that feeling. She said,

> I didn't at first. The *Alien* fantasy, remember? But I like it now. I just worry about getting him out. I can't believe my body will be able to push him out. Oh well, I can't control these things, so I guess I'll just relax. I'm getting scared of the pain. I'm afraid I won't be able to do it. My whole life will be changing. But there's nothing I can do about it. I just can't imagine how it will be. You

> can't know how something you've never experienced will be, and I guess that makes you nervous. And I'm getting so uncomfortable. I don't think I can stand it much longer.

Naomi's seemed more resolved to her husband as delivery approached. She gave up on the three-day work week idea. "He says he wants to be with the baby. But not enough to go to a three-day week. I guess if he wants to get ahead, that's not practical. All I can think about now is the baby. I'm very self-involved. I don't care about anything else. My sexist father was talking about politics, and I wanted to yell at him, but I just couldn't be bothered."

The Friday after this session, I got a call from Naomi. She was crying. "They're going to induce me tonight. At first they said they would give me till Monday to go into labor, but then they said, why wait? So they want to do it tonight. I really don't want to do this, but they say it's best." I said, "Do you feel ready or do you feel rushed?" She said, "I feel rushed. I'm a basket case." I said, "Can you advocate for yourself? Can you tell the doctor you want to wait the weekend and see what happens?" She said, "I don't feel I know enough. Who am I to question the doctor?" I said, "Tell your baby it's time to go into labor."

When she called again, Naomi had had her baby.

> It was horrible and wonderful. When I got to the hospital, I refused to sign the consent forms, because they waived my right to be consulted about anything. Finally they wrote out a document I could sign. They were taking me to the delivery room at eight when I gave birth in the hall. There were no doctors. Next time I'm going with a midwife. It was so thrilling to see that little head sticking out of me. I was out on Sunday. I've been at my mother's ever since. Today on the way home, I started to cry. "Oh my God, I have this beautiful little son."

When she arrived at her next session, Naomi looked tired.

> I'm not doing so good. I just can't believe I'm a mother. I don't feel like a mother yet. Even though he's mine, I don't feel like he came from me. It was the most awesome thing I've ever experienced. I still can't believe I did it. They wanted me to lie down, but I insisted on standing up. And then as they were wheeling me into the delivery room, the baby's head crowned, and I was in a position so I could see it, and it was the most profound moment of my life. I put my hands down and felt the head, and I thought, "Oh my God, it's a baby!" I never really believed till that moment. It was awesome. I'll never forget when I saw his head coming out of my body. We'll never be the same after

> that. It hurt, but it was the most beautiful moment of my life. I can't think about it now without crying. But it's not sadness. I don't know what the tears are about, but it's not sadness.

Naomi struggled in the weeks that followed with the masculine-feminine issues that had preoccupied her before the birth, but there were subtle changes. She was still the feminist complaining that

> Men are so rigid and self-involved. Women are taught to do what they have to do, whether it's enduring pain or being cut. We're trained to take care of and give pleasure. We give and give and never ask to get. Men just aren't trained to serve others. They have no idea how to mother. That's my responsibility, and I resent it. I'm the one who has to make sacrifices. Boys get trucks and blocks and camcorders for their birthdays. Look what we give girls—dolls and toy kitchens. What's the message? You're here to serve. I'm not going to give my best friend's baby girl a doll, even if I did see a beautiful one. Caretaking is held in contempt. You're only worthwhile if you have a career.

But then she added something new: "The truth is that I want to be the one to raise the baby. Why do I feel that I'm only worthwhile if I make a million dollars on Wall Street?" Naomi seemed to be experiencing the idea that she wanted the feminine role and could even find some dignity and authority in such a self-concept.

Part of this new thinking centered on her husband. She seemed to have given up the idea of turning him into a co-mother and decided that women must assume the responsibility in mothering. She said, "He wants to help, but how can he? He's willing, but I'm the one with the breasts." At times, Naomi expressed anger at her husband's inability to be a mother. "He will make no decisions about the baby. He treats me as the authority, and it's very annoying. He never takes care of the baby. He only plays with him." But she added something new: "I used to just passively accept all this stuff, but now I'm going to insist."

If Naomi's relationship with her husband had been altered, changes in her ideas about her mother were even more striking. She still was conflicted about her mother, saying through tears, "I feel so guilty, because she is just exhausted taking care of all of us. I think she's a better mother than I am. She can calm the baby down in a way that I can't. My father would help, but he just doesn't know how." But then she expressed a new idea: "Now I can identify with my mother. I used to see her as self-sacrificing. But now I know. You do it for this strange kind of love. You just love that baby. It's like loving yourself."

In the next session, Naomi made her clearest statement about her conflictual identifications. She said,

> I think I modeled myself after my father. I didn't want to be so self-sacrificing. I got my M.B.A. But now that I'm a mother, I don't have any role model but my mother. My father didn't mother. He was a workaholic. So now that I'm a mother, I can't use my father as a role model. I always used to rail against staying home and being a mother, and now I think, "What's wrong with staying home and taking care of your kid?" We just feel we're not meaningful human beings if we don't have a meaningful career outside the home. But what could be more meaningful than raising a child? We play such roles. In my house growing up, the girls set the table and washed the dishes. The boys raked leaves and mowed the lawn. When we all went to work for my father, my brothers drove trucks, and my sisters and I filed like secretaries.

I asked why she thought her father was so sexist. Naomi said, "My grandmother was very strong. She walked all over my grandfather. My husband comes from the same kind of family. His mother is very strong, and she dominates his father. I guess I'm pretty strong too. I really didn't want to become my mother, and yet, it's not so bad to become your mother. My mother is a good woman. She lived with this sexist man all her life, but she held her own."

In the weeks after the birth, Naomi spoke continuously about being out of control. "I'm so tired. I've lost total control over my life. He doesn't sleep at all, and my career is a joke. I'm going to have to quit my job, I think. I was supposed to go in yesterday, and I just never made it. Here I am, sleepless, jobless, living with my mother, but it's great!" I asked her what was so great about it. She said, "To have someone you love that much. He's a person. He came out of me. I don't feel like I created him. I don't feel like this powerful creator. But it's just something so profound. Pregnancy is just a state of constant metamorphosis. Things are changing and growing all the time. How can you realize any of this before it happens?

A few months later, Naomi decided to go back to work.

> I feel diminished that I'm not bringing money into the family. I'm not cut out to be a full-time mother. It's just not me. I feel like I'm a good mother. I was so worried that I had no maternal instincts, but it all just sort of kicks in naturally. I don't feel nervous now. I could be a full-time mother, but it's just too hard. I need time away or I'll go crazy.

Naomi's mother took care of the baby when she went back to work.

In the next session, Naomi said, "You know, I've been thinking, womanhood is just a wonderful thing. I guess I feel a little sad. Have I ever allowed myself to feel like a woman? But on the other hand, if I had allowed myself to feel like a woman, would I have done anything different? I've been fighting it all my life, but really when I think of what I would have done differently, what? Wearing tops that are cut lower? I really wouldn't have done anything differently. And I've been thinking, maybe it isn't such a bad thing to let little girls have dolls. It teaches them one of the most important parts of life."

Discussion

Naomi's case certainly illustrates the struggle between masculine and feminine identification, which is so common in pregnancy. Her ambivalence about the pregnancy and the tremendous anxiety she was feeling when she came into treatment were expressed in her simple statement, "I'm afraid I'm going to turn into my mother." The fact that Naomi was able to get pregnant so easily was one of many factors that indicated to me that unconsciously there was a lot of libido directed toward her maternal imago. Naomi herself on several occasions verbalized the idea that she got pregnant because she had a "good" and "accepting" mother. It was clear that Naomi loved her mother and felt that she had protected her against her powerful, aggressive father. The mother Naomi was resisting identifying with was the masochistic, passive mother, the one who "totally sacrificed herself to motherhood." Naomi's vomiting early in pregnancy and her sense that the baby was an "alien" were indicative of her aggression toward this troublesome fetus, which was going to turn her into her mother.

Though it was clear that Naomi had a persecuting father and a protecting mother, her identifications were quite complex. Her masculine appearance, her feminism, her wish to make her husband a co-mother, and her desire to be a fireman, an electrician, and a stockbroker indicated that Naomi was identifying with her phallic father. And yet, the paternal imago was not totally dominant or without conflict. Her inner world reflected the outer reality that mother could hold her own against powerful father. Though she valued masculine characteristics, she identified with her mother enough to get pregnant, and like mother, she wanted to raise her baby herself. Her idea that she got pregnant and bought a house she hated in order to please her husband reflected the fact that her masculine imago was so intrapsychically dominant that the self was compelled to take a submissive, a "feminine" position to it. Her choice of her father's doctor and her "I don't know enough" attitude toward the doctor also illustrated this passive stance.

Though Naomi resisted her maternal identification, she also demonstrated a wish to regress to symbiotic union with her mother. She often spoke about her desire to be close to her mother. She seemed to want to eat her mother up when she said, "I need to be close to my mother. I need her, but I feel so guilty about using her. She gave up her life for us." Her desire to "go right to my mother's house" and her "old room," but not to have her mother with her in the room indicated an impulse to return to the womb and be her mother's baby. But again, the maternal identification was not without conflict. Naomi devalued femininity. Dolls and toy kitchens were demeaning symbols of what it means to be female. Serving others and caretaking were perceived as contemptible.

In Naomi's inner world, the self seemed to take a subordinate position to both the maternal and paternal internalized objects. Despite her easy fertility, her feminism, and her wish to "put food on the table," Naomi could be quite passive. Her basic anxiety seemed to express itself when she worried "That I'm going to get in there in labor and not be able to stand up for myself, and things will start happening to me." Caught in a triad where her mother "is a better mother than me" and her father could tell her how to run her life, Naomi was dominated by her internalized objects. Pregnancy and childbirth seemed to effect a positive change on that situation. She said, toward the end of her pregnancy that she was "very self-involved." For the first time, she "just couldn't be bothered" with her father's political harangues. There were suggestions that the pregnancy provided her new insulation against the dominating paternal imago. In the hospital, Naomi took an active stand in a setting that was inducing her to her old passivity. She refused to sign the consent form, refused to lie down, and later decided her next baby would be with a midwife. She said, "I used to just passively accept all this stuff, but now I'm going to insist." After the baby was born, though she complained that "I'm the one with the breasts," that complaint seemed to also contain a boast.

After birth, Naomi was able to identify with her mother in a much more conflict-free way. She said, "Now that I'm a mother, I don't have any role model but my mother. I can't use my father as a role model. Now I can identify with my mother. I used to see her as self-sacrificing. But now I know." Her mother was strong, but "I guess I'm pretty strong too. I really didn't want to become my mother, and yet it's not so bad to become your mother. My mother is a good woman. She lived with this sexist all her life, but she held her own."

How do we understand this positive change in Naomi? I suggest that several shifts in her psychic inner triangle occurred because of her pregnancy. The self became stronger in relation to the parental introjects. The internalized father was no longer dominating the self and the internalized mother. Naomi was able to stop unconsciously competing with her father for power based on the masculine model. Her ability to give birth made her his equal in her unconscious, but on her own terms. She was also more in tune with the maternal introject, and this was due to a phenomenon that I saw over and over in my work with pregnant women. Childbirth seems to modify the nature of the "mother-in-me." A shift of identification occurs. The maternal representation seems to move from an identification with the passive, masochistic mother—who is the heir of the Oedipal complex—and return to the relationship with the original phallic mother of the pre-Oedipal period. But additionally, the relationship with the maternal imago and self alters. The self gives up the submissive stance toward this phallic mother. No longer the baby to the engulfing mother, the woman incorporates the phallic mother within her own ego and experiences true identification with and individuation from the early maternal object. Thus, the original female problem of achieving autonomy while retaining female identification is resolved.

In many ways, Naomi's pregnancy helped her achieve the goal of being both her mother and her father. She did not become the mother who sacrificed her life. Using her more integrated identification with her father, she went back to work full-time. But she also embraced her femininity for the first time after "fighting it all my life." Childbirth helped Naomi get in touch with a uniquely female power and realize that "womanhood is a wonderful thing."

How does pregnancy achieve this new integration of the psychic triangle? An answer to this question lies in an examination of how Naomi experienced her pregnancy. She was full of fear and anxiety throughout most of it. She certainly equated pregnancy with death and danger. She talked about her condition in ways that we talk about death: "My whole life will be changing. There's nothing I can do about it. I just can't imagine how it will be. You can't know how something you've never experienced will be, and I guess that makes you nervous. It's so hard to imagine doing this; to think I'll be doing something I've never done before." I believe the unexplainable tears that are "not sadness," and which are experienced by so many women after birth, are tears in response to the association of death and childbirth. We mourn the loss of infant-self and we weep. Naomi, like many of the women I worked with who had babies, talked about "acceptance," and this is a word often associated with death, dying, and mourning.

Childbirth is a triumph of life over death, and this enormous psychic feat empowers the ego to take charge of the internal triangle and integrate all its aspects into the personality in a constructive way.

Another explanation of this shift in the triangle can be gained by examining Naomi's vacillating cathexes of self and object representations in pregnancy. The early vomiting and the compulsive worry indicated aggression toward the pregnancy and the fetus. Naomi wanted to get rid of the intruder, smother it or poison it with Diet Coke. I believe the "something creepy" growing inside her was her own voracious wish to be totally dependent on her mother, to eat her up. Early in pregnancy, the fetus was the primitive self, threatening Naomi's life with the old fear of engulfing symbiosis. The sonogram made the baby seem "real" to Naomi. When she could perceive him as an object separate from herself, she resolved herself to the pregnancy. She liked to feel her son move and realize he was a real baby. Though it took her a while to "feel like a mother" and "realize he really came from me," Naomi was finally able to experience her female power. She said, "I don't feel like this powerful creator," but there were many indications that on some level, she did. She said, "To think my mother once held me like I hold him. That I was once that little. It touches something very deep." We see in the case of Naomi a progression from identification of fetus with the helpless pre-Oedipal self, to the experience of the fetus as an object which enables the woman to identify with her own phallic mother, thereby triumphing over the powerless self-representation and achieving true individuation from the internalized maternal object.

CHAPTER THREE

Menopause and Beyond: The Emergence of the Self

A woman in her early fifties arrived in my office shortly after her husband told her he was in love with a younger woman and wanted a divorce. She said to me, "The rest of my life is an epilogue. Everything good that is ever going to happen to me has happened. I feel empty."

Though this patient was clearly depressed, her statement is characteristic of many women in menopause. After a lifetime of feeling full, and sometimes feeling unpleasantly full of introjects, menopausal women consistently report a feeling of emptiness. A manic woman who was also going through a divorce described her frantic, fragmented life as "exhausting. Sometimes I wish I could stop going to the gym and attending committee meetings and having lunches with people I don't really care about. But I'm afraid of what I will find if I give myself time to look inside. Because really I'm just a big blank, a meaningless void at bottom."

Bemesderfer (1996) described the prototypical fantasy of menopause as a sense that the ovaries are shriveling or shrinking, and that one has a cavity or hollow space where the reproductive organs used to be. This sense of being "emptied out," as another patient described it, is a unique feeling for a woman. Throughout the life cycle, her intrapsychic life has been alive with introjects. From the original incorporation of the pre-Oedipal mother and the internalization of the Oedipal father, and continuing through the multitude of projections and fantasies of pregnancy, childbirth, and motherhood; the overriding theme of female development has been the internalization of and identification with objects.

Of course, the common fantasy of psychic emptiness at the menopause is due in part to a woman's actual situation at this point in her life. The end of bleeding and all the uncomfortable symptoms of menopause are rooted in the body and demand in a way that cannot be ignored or denied, that a woman is losing her sexual powers and that ultimately, she will age and die. Her once powerful parents are also either aging or dying. Husbands, lovers, and children, who have provided opportunities for all sorts of projections, introjections, and fantasies, are gone or at least are making fewer demands. Looked at from this perspective, inner emptiness can be the expression of a harsh reality of loneliness and a feeling of expendability.

But to stop there, and to say that reality is sufficient explanation for the fantasy of emptiness, is to place woman in the familiar role of masochistic victim, so beloved by feminists and psychoanalysts. It discounts the psychoanalytic theory of motivation. After all, the experience of psychic emptiness is a fantasy created by the woman who is feeling empty. Why in the face of her situation does she not intensify her cathexes to all those objects she has fantasized inside her? Why does she expel them all out of her mind in a great burst of psychic housecleaning? The instinctual energy, required for this banishment of internalized objects, gives lie to the idea that everything is over at menopause.

Psychoanalysis has traditionally been firmly pessimistic about the prospects of therapeutic intervention in the aging patient. Freud (1905, 264), writing about who is fit to treat, asserted that "near or above the age of fifty, the elasticity of the mental processes on which the treatment depends is, as a rule, lacking. Old people are no longer educable." He was even grimmer in his evaluation when he focused on women: "A woman of thirty often frightens us by her psychical rigidity and unchangeablity. Her libido has taken up final positions and seems incapable of exchanging them for others. There are no paths open to further development; it is as though the whole process has already run its course and remains henceforth insusceptible to influence—as though, indeed, the difficult development to femininity has exhausted the possibilities of the person concerned" (Freud 1933, 134–35).

Freud's (1913) description of the menopausal woman is even more bleak:

> it is a well known fact and one that has given much ground for complaint, that after women have lost their genital function, their character often undergoes a peculiar alteration, they become quarrelsome, vexacious, and over-bearing, petty and stingy, that is to say that they exhibit typically sadistic and anal-erotic traits which they did not possess earlier during their period of womanliness. We can see that this alteration of character corresponds to a regression of

> sexual life to the pre-genital sadistic and anal erotic stage in which we have discovered the disposition to obsessional neurosis. (323–24)

Freud (1912; 1917; 1926) asserted that menopause can increase the strength of the instincts and impoverish the ego in a way that can cause a neurosis in an otherwise normal woman or, at the very least, can lead to an enormous disruption in the equilibrium of mental health. The increase in libido that occurs during this period often has fewer opportunities for discharge and therefore is repressed and converted into anxiety. Women become afraid of dying, going mad, or having a stroke.

Deutsch (1924, 56) called menopause "an incurable narcissistic wound." She described a process in which the libido, without possibility of cathexis and with a diminished capacity for sublimation, regresses to abandoned infantile positions. If this is true, if there are no further possibilities for growth, it is no wonder that women are depressed at the climacteric.

The stage of menopause is unquestionably a psychic crisis in the life of a woman, perhaps the most challenging she will ever face. Described as a partial death (Deutsch 1945, 459), it most certainly is a confrontation with death, and to survive this face-off requires the creative mobilization, not only of libido but also of all the aggression which a woman possesses. This is a particular challenge, because it is very likely that the menopausal woman has been told all her life that aggression is "unfeminine," and that buying into that idea has bought her considerable political power in her dealings with the opposite sex. With the cessation of the menses, she finds herself losing that power. Often this situation results in a feeling of being cheated. "I have been good all my life," said my abandoned patient, "I loved my husband, and I sacrificed myself for my children, and what do I have to show for it? Nothing! I'm all alone facing old age and death by myself."

Just as in adolescence, there is a surge of both libido and aggression in menopause. But clinically, menopausal women almost always present as depressed. Freud (1917) described depression as the expression of sadism and hate, originally directed at an object, turned around upon the subject's own self. The ego treats itself as an object and directs all the murderous impulses originally aimed at objects in the external world toward the self. A woman experiencing all the troubling physical symptoms of menopause, even if she has never been depressed, will typically begin to focus aggression on her self, seeing herself as used up and worthless. She will mourn the loss of the beautiful, young girl she once was, with a concurrent sense of humiliation and shame.

This depressive reaction at the climacteric, though similar to the melancholia and mourning process that Freud described, has unique characteristics that are related to the reworking of the internal triangle that occurs at menopause. The menopausal woman's reactive depression is more than just self-attack: it is also an assault on her complex internal world of introjected objects. Cleavens (1976, 140) painted a picture of the depressive as a lonely person who is never really alone: "His internal objects are always with him, affording some comfort even while they criticize." Certainly female human beings take comfort in their internalized objects: The mastery and control women achieve on a fantasy level by setting up the internal triangle and reworking it through the life cycle are primary motivators for the establishment and maintenance of the intricate endopsychic world typical of women. But with the dramatic events of the climacteric—not only the hot flashes, weight gain, and sleeplessness but also the disappearance of significant objects—women tend to attempt, on a fantasy level, to empty themselves of the complex system of internal objects that has been with them for most of their lives.

The expulsion of internalized objects, which results in the sense of psychic emptiness at the climacteric, is fueled by an enormous amount of unconscious aggression. The picture that menopausal women present in the treatment room of emptiness and depression reflects this expulsion and the focus of bound aggression on the self. Redirecting this psychic aggressive energy away from the self and out into the object world where it can be used in creative ways becomes the goal of treatment. Once the aggression, which has been turned against the self, can be liberated into words, the bound libido that Freud and Deutsch described as making women neurotic or infantile is also free to find creative outlets. The triumph of menopause, if all goes well, is an ascendancy of the self over the myriad and complex introjections and identifications of the female psyche. Let us examine some of these internalized objects and their fate at the menopause.

The Maternal Imago

As in every crisis of female development, menopause is a confrontation with the original mother. The loss of reproductive function at menopause is a symbolic castration that unconsciously reactivates the rage at the mother which initiated the female Oedipal conflict. Just as in the Oedipal and adolescent periods, when young girls are dealing with a heightened sense of penis envy, castration anxiety in menopause once again mobilizes aggression toward and a strong sense of identification with the Oedipal mother. Echoing a theme of pregnancy, a menopausal woman will verbalize a fear of "becoming my mother." A fifty-five-year-old female patient came in for a session one day and instead of taking the couch, she glared at me and said, "I look in the mirror these days, and I see my mother. I'm beginning to look just like my mean old mother. How are you going to help me with that? I've been working with you for six years to get that sadist out of my head, and now here she is again—the old lady in my mirror. I can't stand it!"

The weight gain that typically accompanies the climacteric is often associated with this fear of becoming the mother. A female patient told me she had gained thirty-five pounds in three years. She was so depressed about it that she was having trouble going out into the world. She refused to buy new clothes and spent all her time at home in her pajamas. She said, "You don't understand what this means to me. I have always been petite. I was my father's little doll. It was my mother who was the plump cow. I can't believe this is happening to me." Though insisting she was not suicidal ("I would never do that to my daughter. She would never get over it."), she told me, "My father died at seventy-two, but my mother died at sixty-six. I look like my mother now. I just hope I take after her in dying young." This statement expresses both aggression toward and identification with the aging mother.

The maternal imago has served a woman well through the vicissitudes of the Oedipal conflict, adolescence, pregnancy and childbirth, and motherhood. Identification with the powerful mother of the pre-Oedipal period has allowed her to see herself as possessed of a phallic energy, as the creator and sustainer of life. Losing her fertility makes this identification harder, and this threatens to alter the maternal imago in a detrimental way. The powerful, full-of-milk mother is becoming "the old lady in the mirror."

The Paternal Imago

The renewed identification with and anxiety about the mother often results in a heightened unconscious desire to identify with the internalized father. Menopause is usually characterized by a victory of more masculine traits, such as aggression and assertiveness, over the feminine qualities of passivity and empathy. Greer (1991, 50) talked about the "virilization" that accompanies old age. Estrogen, depleted during menopause, suppresses anger, so a new and uncomfortable rage is a common menopausal symptom. Also common is a more masculine assertiveness: menopause, as nature's contraceptive (59), frees women for leadership roles in the family and community more often reserved for men. Menopausal women speak of a new freedom to "say what's on my mind without worrying so much what other people feel."

Aggression and libido take on a more masculine quality for women at the climacteric. Rather than waiting passively to be loved, the menopausal woman turns libido outward to the object world to "gild every grass blade and bless every fly." The older woman's love is not focused on herself, nor on herself in the mirror of her lover's eyes, nor is it as corrupted by need as earlier (Greer 1991, 10). For the first time in her life, she may find herself wooing rather than being wooed. She loves and pursues younger objects, both male and female. A sixty-five-year-old woman told me she no longer goes to a club where she used to regularly have lunch. She said, "It's so depressing over there. Everyone is pushing eighty. I feel like I'm in God's waiting room!" Instead, she methodically cultivated younger friends, making lunch dates and courting them as a young man would a young woman.

Heightened penis envy at the climacteric can also take the form of a specific kind of aggression toward men. Fifty-year-old men may be aging but they can still make babies, so their reproductive potency is not threatened in the manifest way that the cessation of bleeding signals the end of fecundity for women. Envy of this phallic potency provides the energy to reconfigure a menopausal woman's relationship to all the males in her life. This reconfiguration is usually most clearly focused on husbands or partners.

The climacteric can be a dangerous stage for a marriage. Early in a marriage, a wife often experiences her husband as the idealized phallic father, the object who at last can give her the wished for penis and child. Pregnancy and birth give a woman a symbolic phallus of her own, which can disrupt this idealization of the husband. When children are gone and fertility ceases, a woman may see her partner in a new light. A woman who had left her husband told the group, "I never really noticed that I didn't like him that much, that he made me really angry. I was too focused on getting those babies from him and then raising them. But after the last one went to college, I looked at him and realized that I just didn't need him anymore."

Evolving Relationships to Children

Of course, it is not only husbands who are leaving or being expelled. If a woman has had children, she is now face-to-face with the tragic destiny of motherhood: her children are growing up and separating to begin their own lives, and she is no longer psychically inhabited with them. For years, her child has been both self and object. Indeed, it has been possible to live through her children. Motherhood has kept her relatively comfortable and busy as a receiving station for her children's affective impulses. They, in turn, have very helpfully been the external port for all her fantasies and projections. As her children mature, a woman must learn to see them as separate objects not under her control. Her libido, which has been utilized for motherly nurturance and tenderness, as well as the aggression which fueled a mother's fierce protectiveness, no longer have an outlet. Though intuitively, most "good enough" mothers understand that they must break their symbiotic tie with their children, it almost always feels like a narcissistic injury.

The growth of children can be experienced in the female unconscious as the death of children, and this loss must be mourned at the menopause. The repetition compulsion manifests as a longing for the past and for the little children who will never come back—and whose disappearance is just as sad as the prospect of never having known these children at all. Life and death instincts, expressed on the one hand as a progressive tendency to aid the child in his development and free her own ego from the tyranny of motherhood, and on the other by a wish to restore the prenatal unity and preserve the psychic umbilical cord, struggle, with neither achieving a complete victory (Deutsch 1945).

Grown children can remobilize the old relationships with parents preserved in the internal triangle. There can be a flight from a son just as pronounced as the flight from the father at the end of the Oedipal period (Deutsch, 1945); for the same reason: Like the father, the son is likely to be embroiled in a sexual relationship, which places his mother firmly on the outside, looking in. Adult daughters, with their ability to grow and suckle babies, can reignite the resentment toward the pre-Oedipal mother. Watching a grown daughter with her own children can remind a woman that menopause ends a woman's service to the species—and this is a mortification to feminine narcissism (Deutsch 1945).

The only way for a woman to preserve her tie to her children after they become adults is to try to identify with their life interests. But this is meager recompense for losing control over their lives. The loss of the possibility of bearing any more children debilitates a crucial female tendency: the ability to introject objects and use them. As in the Oedipal period and adolescence, the female human being must mobilize all the forces of her ego to adjust to reality and turn her psychic energy toward new goals. The wish to bear a child must be sublimated to other procreative goals. If all goes well, libido and aggression are redirected, and the urge to intellectual and artistic achievement replaces the productivity of motherhood. Creative impulses that have been muted by marriage and motherhood return.

The Expulsion of Internalized Objects

The almost universal complaint of "emptiness" in the menopausal woman reflects an unconscious psychic dynamic functioning in response to the challenges of the climacteric. Throughout their adulthood, female human beings use the internal triangle to inform their relationships with the objects in their lives. We have seen how pregnant women project all sorts of fantasies that have to do with the maternal and paternal introjects onto their unborn babies. The internal triangle colors relationships with all the important objects in a woman's life. Feelings about husbands and lovers and sons are filtered through the fantasy of the internalized father. Daughters and female friends are perceived through the lens of the maternal introject.

With the crisis of menopause, identification with the fertile mother which has proved so helpful to her is no longer possible. Identification with the aging mother—the "old lady in the mirror"—is a wound to her diminished ego. The introjected mother has served its purpose and is no longer useful. On the level of fantasy, then, the maternal introject is expelled from the psyche. This expulsion is fueled by aggression and is part of the regression to infantile positions, the anal-sadistic fantasies that Freud described.

Whereas in pregnancy and childbirth the goal was to identify with the internalized mother in new and powerful ways, the goal at the climacteric is to free the patient from her identification with the mother and help her verbalize the ways she is *different* from her mother.

The fantasy rejection and expulsion of the maternal introject sets up a less ambivalent relation to the paternal imago. The internalized father is useful to the menopausal woman when all hope of identifying with the phallic mother is gone. Identification with this introject is responsible for the "virilization" that is typical of menopause. Despite the utility of the male introject, there is likely to be enormous aggression directed toward it too. The aging woman is losing her sexual powers and most of the men in her life—whether they are abandoning or disappointing fathers and husbands or unfaithful sons—are rejecting her. In this way, they resemble the father who was introjected at the end of the Oedipal period: There is no possibility of either the penis or a child from any of them. And there is another problem. When the internalized mother is expelled from the psyche, there is a real danger that the remaining paternal introject will overwhelm the ego. This unconscious fantasy of the ego being attacked by a male imago is one of the dynamics of the reactive depression so common at the menopause.

The vacillation between identification with and aggression toward the paternal introject plays itself out clinically as a conflict between depression and rage. The intrapsychic attack on the ego by the male imago expresses itself in feelings of worthlessness and sexual expendability. The identification with that same imago gives women the spurt of aggressive masculine energy which can prove so helpful at the climacteric. Ironically, it is probably the identification with the phallic introject and his masculine energy that finally fuels his expulsion from the female psyche.

The reactive depression of menopause, with its concurrent "sense of emptiness" reflects an intrapsychic conflict, having to do with the internal triangle. The maternal introject is banished, and the female ego tends to subvert itself to the paternal imago which remains. The ego mourns the loss of the comforting "mother-in-me," causing a fantasy of emptiness and worthlessness. This self-attack is facilitated by an equally strong fantasy of the ego's humiliation by the internal father who remains. The conflict between identification with and subversion to the paternal imago is where the clinical work at the menopause plays itself out. Aging women must be aided in their struggle with the imago of the father. Just as in pregnancy when a woman learns to identify in a new way with the phallic mother who gives birth, a menopausal woman must work toward an identification with a phallic male energy, which can help her set her life on a new path toward creative, procreative outlets in the world. And as in pregnancy and childbirth, a new kind of identification with the internalized father can help her separate from the oppression of the ego by this paternal imago.

A lesbian woman in my menopause group listened impatiently to all the other women complain of depression and emptiness. This gay woman had had a very intense identification to her father within all along, and she said, "Empty! You're not empty. You have yourself. That's what the challenge of menopause is, ladies. You're going to have to finally learn to take care of yourselves!"

The Case of Bess

Bess, a fifty-two-year-old woman, came into treatment at the suggestion of family court. She was separated from her husband of twenty-five years and had gotten an order of protection against him from the court. She told me that she and her husband had never had an argument until a month before she came to my office, when they had had such a bitter quarrel that he picked up a knife and threatened her with it. She threw him out of the house and called a lawyer. She was not sure whether she wanted to divorce him. All she knew was that she liked having him out of the house. Her husband had been unemployed for five years and Bess's salary as a schoolteacher had been their sole source of income. Bess told me

> I used to come home after working all day, and there Ralph would be in his underwear watching reality television. His clothes and papers were everywhere,

> and he would look at me and say, "What's for dinner?" I did the laundry, the housework, paid the bills. And I was the only one who was working!

Bess and Ralph had a twenty-year-old son, away at college, who had major learning disabilities. Bess told me that she had been the boy's tutor and coach throughout his childhood. It was clear that she had been very attached to her son.

> When he had troubles at school, it broke my heart. Ralph said I babied him too much, and maybe I did. I admit that I wrote some of those high school papers for him, and God—when he took the SAT, I fought to get him an untimed test, and we went over vocabulary for months. Sometimes I resented it, but what could I do? I couldn't bear to see him suffer.

Bess told me that it had been hard for her to separate from her son when he went off to college. Despite the fact that he was attending a special school for learning-disabled students and was being tutored, Bess called him every day and wanted to help him write his papers. She nagged him about which courses he should be taking and how he should schedule his studies. Shortly before her argument with Ralph, Bess's son had told her to stop calling and leave him alone.

Since her husband had left, Bess was having upsetting fantasies that Ralph and her son were spying on her and plotting against her to have her evicted from the family apartment. She had confronted her son about these fears and he had told her that she was having "crazy paranoid fantasies." This did nothing to reassure Bess, who was convinced that her neighbors had joined her husband and son in a plot to destroy her. In the sessions, she obsessed about the plots against her in a rigid and repetitive manner.

Bess also told me about her difficult mother. A frustrated actress with an alcoholic husband, her mother took no joy in her children. Bess was not allowed to have birthday parties or invite friends over after school. Her mother hated the house they lived in, though she was terrified of ending up homeless. She had no friends, telling Bess, "I am not a joiner." She constantly complained about money and warned Bess that if she didn't curb her spending, they would all end up "out in the street." Her mother criticized Bess's hair, her figure, and her personality and she expected her daughter to "earn her keep." Bess cleaned bathrooms and scrubbed floors from the time she was six years old. Her mother told her she was preparing her for her life as a wife and mother. And indeed, Bess said that the only time her mother seemed genuinely pleased with her was when she married Ralph and became a "respectable woman." Her father, despite his alcoholism, seemed to be a more nurturing figure. He fought with his wife, who saw no need for Bess to go to college. He prevailed and the father paid for her education.

Bess's life in her marriage echoed her life with her mother. Soon after she married Ralph, she settled into the role of "wife and slave." She moved into Ralph's apartment, but he did nothing to make her feel welcome. His closets were filled with the beat-up furniture he had inherited from his parents, and she was able to bring only "one little chair" from her old apartment. They placed it in the bedroom and whenever Bess complained about being mistreated, Ralph told her to "go sit in your chair and leave me alone." Bess was once again scrubbing floors and earning her keep. She said, "Ralph didn't really marry me. He hired me to take care of him."

Bess's father had died of a brain tumor a few years before she came into treatment. Bess was so upset during the final stages of his illness that she couldn't visit him in the hospital. "He died alone," she told me, "Neither my mother or I were there when he died." Shortly after her father's death, Bess developed strange symptoms—migraine headaches, shortness of breath, diarrhea, and gas. She had always been very healthy, but now she took herself from doctor to doctor taking all sorts of tests. No one could find anything wrong with her, but Bess was convinced she was dying. When a doctor told her she was perfectly healthy, she said that she must have some disease. In exasperation, the doctor said, "What kind of disease would you like to have?" He recommended Bess see a psychiatrist, which she did. This doctor put her on an antianxiety medication and all her symptoms went away. Bess said, "I still struggle with my fears though. I'm convinced I'm going to die of cancer like my father."

Bess told me that when she began to have the physical symptoms of menopause, she lost all interest in sex. This upset Ralph very much, but Bess was unmoved, "I just didn't want him to touch me." She also reported that since Ralph had left, her sexuality had come flooding back. "I masturbate all the time now," she said.

Whenever I asked Bess about her thoughts and feelings, she said, "Thoughts? I don't have any thoughts. And I guess I don't really know what a feeling is."

One of the most difficult aspects of the treatment was Bess's tendency to go into what she called "one of my downward spirals." If a challenge presented itself, such as a fight with her son or an unpleasant talk with Ralph, Bess would begin to cry and have fantasies about her own destruction. She became convinced that she would end up poor, alone, out on the street in the snow. These spells could last for several days. When she was in the throes of one, she would call my office—often in the middle of the night—and leave a message on my voice mail which was nothing but inarticulate sobbing. When I returned her call the next day, she seemed outraged that I had not been there to receive her call at four in the morning. She was stony and punishing on the phone and when she would come in for her session, she presented as an abused victim of my lack of concern for her. She equated these difficult spells with the symptoms of menopause: migraine headaches, sleeplessness, and particularly the hot flashes. She said, "When I get like this, I burn! I burn!" She complained of waking in the middle of the night drenched in sweat, saying, "It's like I'm trying to get rid of something."

A year into the treatment, Bess's mother became ill. Now Bess was spending most of her free time tending to her mother's needs. During this period, she became aware of a feeling: She reported that she was angry at her mother and wished that she would die so that she could enjoy her money. Bess was terribly ashamed of this anger, and we worked for several months on the idea that rage is just a feeling and probably a justified feeling in this case. When her mother died, Bess decided that she would divorce her husband and she started proceedings against him.

As Bess became more comfortable with her own aggression, several positive things happened. The "downward spirals" became less frequent and then disappeared. I had suggested to Bess that when she felt one of these spells coming on, she should try to figure out who she was angry at. This seemed to give her some control over these episodes. Another good development was that Bess began to develop some ideas. She had always wanted to take piano lessons but Ralph had told her they couldn't afford to buy a piano. Now she bought a small upright and began lessons. She began to talk about a new feeling, the pleasure she felt when she made music.

Bess joined a book club, began to work out at a gym, and seemed to be enjoying a new control working with a lawyer to get the best settlement in her divorce. Clearly, her life was getting better. But her paranoid fantasy that her son and her husband were plotting against her remained entrenched, a pocket of immovable pathology, despite the many improvements she had made. She also began to be obsessed with the idea that she was turning into her dead mother. Talking about "the old lady in the mirror," Bess would assault her own person, "I am ugly, just like her. I have a big nose and little squinty eyes, just like her. Look at this body! I have a big belly and a frumpy ass, just like her. I have her awful, ugly hair. I am becoming my mother."

I worked with Bess during this period to help her articulate ways she was *unlike* her mother. Her mother never ventured from home. She would never take piano lessons. She would never join a book club. She had stayed with an abusive husband, while Bess had had the courage to divorce hers. Bess described the dowdy, worn clothes that her mother always wore and compared her drab wardrobe to that of her mother. When her divorce was final, Bess began to spend more money on clothes, better haircuts, and makeup. She asked for and got a raise at work.

Despite all these gains, Bess was still convinced that her ex-husband and son were out to get her. When she would present her paranoid fantasies to me in an obsessive, repetitive way, I felt assaulted, just as she had felt assaulted by her mother and Ralph. This symptom seemed depressingly immovable and, at one point, Bess refused to answer her son's calls, "I devoted my whole life to him, and this is the thanks I get. I hate him, and I don't trust him."

Bess wanted to lose the weight she had gained during menopause and she joined Weight Watchers. She had become something of a hermit after Ralph left, enjoying getting home after work and not having to "be hassled by anyone. I can make what I like for dinner. Everything is neat and clean, and I sit and watch television and cuddle with the cat." She claimed she had no wish to have people in her life. But after joining Weight Watchers, she developed a small group of new friends. One of the women that she met was a Buddhist and encouraged an interest in spiritual pursuits. Her friend introduced her to a meditation group and Bess began to meditate every day. In the months that followed, Bess lost forty pounds and began to talk about turning her life over to "a higher power."

One day, Bess came into her session and told me that her anxiety about her ex-husband and son had disappeared. She gave the credit for this development to her spirituality. The meditation and the idea of "letting go and letting God" had freed her from her paranoia. Though happy at this turn of events, I was also angry at Bess for giving no credit to me or the treatment. In fact she said, "Meditation was able to fix me in a way that you have been totally inadequate to do."

Several years into the treatment, Beth reported the following fantasy:

> When I wake up in the morning, before I am really awake, I have this strange sensation. I feel like I'm floating all alone in space. I experience myself as a tiny, tiny person all alone in a big bed in a bigger apartment in a huge city. All this space around me. I feel so small in a huge empty space. And it's not like I'm on cloud nine. It's not like I died and went to heaven. It's very, very lonely and frightening.

At this point, I suggested to Bess that she go into a women's group. I told her I thought she had made tremendous gains in individual treatment, and that group would be the next step in her growth. Though anxious and ambivalent, Bess agreed to try a group. In group sessions, she presented in a whole new way, not the abused victim she was in individual sessions. Instead, she seemed critical, impatient, intolerant, and bored. She came for two sessions, but on the third, she told the group she was leaving. In her individual sessions, she told me she hated the group and all the people in it. She also told me how much she hated me for putting her in the group. "You have plans for me that I don't have for myself," she said, "You just don't understand. I *like* being alone. I don't like people. I like my cat. I don't want to marry again, and I have all the friends I want, and I certainly don't need a group." Later, she modified this stance, telling me, "I guess I just wasn't ready to deal with people." I joined her, saying I had rushed her, imposing my goals instead of understanding hers.

At this point in the treatment, Bess reported a dream:

> I was in a room that I didn't recognize, lying on some sort of table. I looked down at my vagina, and I saw that I had my period. I was passing a blood clot, and I tried to clean myself with a tissue. Then I felt an urge to push, as if I were giving birth. When I pushed, a long, tongue-like creature came out of my vagina. It moved to a corner of the room. I was repulsed and ashamed, but I also felt somewhat attracted to this creature. It moved like a cat, or maybe a dog. Anyway, this creature realized that I was repulsed by it, and it wiggled toward the door to leave. But as it got to the door, it looked back at me and decided to stay.

Bess told me that she had had this birth dream before, but in the past, the newborn had looked more like a shelled lobster tail. She said, "It seems this baby is much different."

Discussion

Bess's treatment began with the literal expulsion of a real object. After years of a marriage in which feelings of anger and resentment had been repressed, she got rid of her husband in a dramatic burst of anal-sadistic rage. Yet Bess felt no conscious anger. Though she had taken out a court order to protect herself from Ralph and to ensure that he would never be able to come home again, she was confused and unsure that she wanted to divorce him. All she reported was emptiness—no thoughts and no feelings.

Through all the years of her marriage, Bess was clearly oppressed by her maternal introject. As her mother had seen her, so she saw herself—as a "wife and slave," someone to scrub the floors and "earn her keep." In her marriage to Ralph, she had chosen an object which allowed her to repeat this masochistic submission. When Ralph threatened her with a knife, she was able to mobilize the aggression frozen in her masochism and eject him from her life. Since Ralph had "hired" Bess rather than loved her, and related to her much as her mother had, his actual banishment was also a symbolic attempt to expel the maternal introject. The difficulty of ridding herself of the toxic maternal object was one reason Bess had to banish Ralph so dramatically; no ambivalence could be entertained against the overwhelming mother he represented.

Bess's "downward spirals" were interesting examples of her relationship with the sadistic mother within. These spirals expressed both love and hate toward the internalized mother. Libido expressed itself in an unconscious identification with her mother: Like her mother, she tortured herself with ideas of being poor and homeless. Aggression was clearly focused on her own ego; there was no doubt that Bess suffered terribly in these episodes. But also like her mother, she tortured the object. These hysterical spells allowed Bess to show me how it felt to be her mother's victim. In the transference, I felt obliterated, wiped out, defective, and useless when she surrendered to despair. Bess's attacks on her own looks were yet another example of how she used her unconscious identification with her mother to attack both the maternal introject and herself. As treatment progressed, and Bess was able to point out my inadequacies rather than torture me with hysteria, I understood that she was projecting her aggression toward the ugly, aging mother/self out onto me in a therapeutic expulsion of the toxic object.

The hot flashes and night sweats of menopause were associated in Bess's mind with anger ("I burn! I burn!") and a wish to get rid of something. I had the idea that what she was struggling to free herself from was the oppression of the maternal imago within. But it wasn't until Bess's actual mother got sick and needed care that Bess was able to give up playing the masochistic victim and let herself feel that she would like to see her mother dead. I found it interesting that only after her mother did die was Bess able to know that she also wanted to get rid of Ralph, the actual object that had played the role of her oppressive maternal imago.

The fantasized expulsion of the maternal introject, following the actual death of her mother and the divorce from Ralph, helped Bess redirect aggression away from her own ego and freed the libido, which had been trapped in unconscious identification with the abusing object. With Ralph, the representative of her toxic mother within, gone, Bess's sexuality flooded back. The freeing of instinctual energy focused on her maternal introject allowed

Bess to study the piano, join a book club, and lose weight. But the victory over the mother within was only a partial one. Bess often regressed to identification with the toxic introject and self-attack, assaulting "the old lady in the mirror."

Part of the work of extricating the maternal imago from her psyche was reflected in the paranoid fantasies Bess developed. Melanie Klein (1932) wrote about the paranoid position, a form of object relating in infancy, which involves splitting a partial object (usually the mother's breast) into the good object and the bad object. The projection of the "bad breast" into external objects can lead to paranoid fantasies. Klein's theory is helpful in thinking about Bess's paranoid symptoms. In a typical menopausal regression to infantile positions, Bess worked to eject the bad breast (the representative of the toxic maternal introject) out of her psyche and project it into her husband and son with her conviction that they were plotting against her. It seemed to me that the persistence and obsessive quality of her paranoid fantasy about her husband and son could also be understood as a fantasy of the male introject attacking her ego. Paranoia is related to obsession and the drive discharge characteristic of the anal period (Freud 1912), and the whole paranoid ideation that Bess developed during this period seemed to be a rigid and immovable obsession that had anal-sadistic characteristics.

The relationship Bess had had with her son while he was growing up was characterized by symbiotic merging. Bess seemed to see the boy as her own victimized self and she took care of him as she wished her mother had cared for her. After her son went to college, she tried to maintain the psychic umbilical cord, but when he refused to cooperate with his mother's plan, she began to have paranoid fantasies. Rather than experiencing the aggression she felt toward her husband and son, she projected it into them and decided that they were plotting against her. This operation illustrated Bess's usual defense against her aggression: She projected it onto objects and experienced them turning her into a victim of their abuse. In the transference, Bess used her rigid paranoid ideas to assault me with the idea that I was defective, just as her mother had assaulted her.

It was interesting to me that though Bess said she loved her father and was terribly upset about his cancer, she let him "die alone." It was around the time of her father's death that Bess lost all sexual interest in Ralph and didn't want him to touch her. Though she had "no feelings," I was quite sure that Bess harbored repressed rage against her father and husband and, on the level of fantasy, toward the paternal imago within. After her father's death, she began to have physical symptoms and fear she too would die of cancer. This turn of events expressed a relationship of love and hate to the paternal introject which was similar to the one she had with the imago of her mother. In identification with the paternal introject, she turned unconscious aggression against her own ego, making herself sick.

The work of Bess's analysis seemed to be the expulsion of the toxic maternal introject from the ego and the reworking of her fantasized relationship with the paternal imago. It was interesting to me that Bess was finally able to overcome her paranoia when she "let go and let God." She seemed to use the idea of God as an idealized phallic father who could take control and save her from the plotting of her husband and son. When she gave the power over to this idealized father, she felt safe enough to give up her paranoid ideation. Identifying with the phallic father within, she projected her own castration anxiety onto me in the transference, telling me how inadequate and impotent I had been to help her.

The fantasy of floating alone in space reflected the psychic emptiness of menopause, but I was mistaken to think that Bess was telling me she wanted to be tethered with connection to other people. Because Bess described herself as frightened and lonely, I missed the pleasure in this fantasy. Only later did I understand that "floating all alone" could be interpreted as a fantasy of freedom from the oppressive internal triangle within. Bess *liked* being alone; she could only experience objects as abusive and sadistic. I suggested a group too soon. I was out of sync with my patient, but it was instructive to see how identified Bess still was with the toxic mother. Like her mother, she hated most other people and was not a "joiner." Her rejection of my group was also an example of how she liked to project her fantasy of a worthless, defective self onto me.

Bess's dream is rich in symbolism. Beginning with bleeding at the beginning of the dream, which I saw as the symbolic castration women so often fantasize at the menopause, it moves to the birth of a strange object, both repelling and friendly. This long tongue-like creature represented a phallus to me. Bess had given birth to the idea of a new, virile, creative self, and though the idea was somewhat repulsive to her, there was also the idea that she could make friends with this new phallic creature. The birth of this phallus had resonances of what childbirth helps a woman achieve. Bess, on a fantasy level, pushed her phallic paternal introject into the world, simultaneously identifying with his power and separating herself from his oppression. Unlike the lobsters with thick shells that Bess had dreamed before, this baby seemed much less defended and walled off.

Menopause is characterized by an ascendancy of the self over the myriad and complex introjections and identifications of the female psyche. Hardly a rehearsal for death, it is a life-and-death struggle, which, if all goes well, results in a new autonomy. The tyranny of the internal triangle is over. Germaine Greer (1991, 110) described the menopausal woman as "a moon without an earth." Now likely alone and unwanted in reality and emptied of all internal objects on a fantasy level, she is also free. She must give up being someone else's daughter, wife, or mother, so that at last she can become *just herself*. This autonomous self is at last emancipated to become the subject of experience and the object of its own care.

Beyond Menopause

Recently, I have had opportunity to analyze postmenopausal women. Several of my patients, who have been with me ten years or more, are now in their seventies or eighties, and I have also observed my own mother and aunts as they face the challenges of aging. These remarkable women belie Freud's ideas about there being no more paths of development open to elderly women. On the contrary, female psychic energy is still reconfiguring in even advanced old age and infirmity. And once again, as in every phase of female development, women confront their mothers.

The process of growing old, particularly when it is combined with illness and infirmity, undoubtedly causes regression. We have all seen elderly people who seem quite childlike. Letting go of authority and control and allowing oneself to be helped is one of the great challenges of old age, but it is interesting to watch the healing that can occur when the transition from feeling influential and powerful to submissive acceptance occurs. On this journey of regression—sometimes to infantile and even intrauterine experience as death approaches—women once again come face-to-face with the powerful pre-Oedipal mother—and even at this late date, the meeting can be therapeutic.

The Case of Bianca

Bianca, a seventy-five-year-old woman, came into treatment with me fifteen years ago after the death of her husband, a novelist. Bianca had tried a group for women in mourning, but she had hated it. "They want me to talk about my feelings," she said, "I don't want to have any feelings." She refused to lie on the couch and waved away my questions about her childhood and her thoughts about her late husband. She made it very clear that all she wanted to talk about were books she had read, movies she had seen, and the quirks of the ladies she had lunch with, all of whom "find me extremely entertaining. I wish I could say the same about them."

For fifteen years, Bianca has been coming to her session with pieces of paper clutched in her hand. She reads me articles from the *New York Times* written by people who agree with her own politics. She recites the poetry she has written. She shares letters from friends she finds amusing. She critiques at length the plays and concerts she has seen, and sometimes even brings a tape recorder to her session to play me music she enjoys. I say practically nothing and often feel that this treatment is useless, but Bianca has a very positive transference to me. She sees me as one of the few people in her life with taste and a discriminating perception about politics and people, though I have never revealed my thoughts about anything to her. From time to time, she tells me how lonely she is and that our sessions are keeping her alive.

A few years ago, Bianca's ninety-nine-year-old mother died. She argued with her brother before her mother's death. The brother wanted to let the mother die in peace but Bianca wanted to do everything possible to keep the mother alive. When the mother died, Bianca blamed her brother. After a lifetime of being very close to her only sibling, she refused to see her brother. These events threatened Bianca's defenses and, briefly, she began to share her grief, telling me that her mother and her late husband were the only people on this earth worthy of her love, and since they were both gone, her life was over. But this encounter with her feelings of pain was only temporary. Soon, Bianca was back to reading editorials and analyzing the various film versions of *Jane Eyre*.

Recently, Bianca came into her session and told me she had taken old movies starring Nelson Eddy and Jeanette MacDonald out of the library to watch. "They make me weep," she told me. I asked her if the movies are sad.

> They're not sad at all. They're just old-fashioned musicals. They're sweet. I don't know why they make me cry, but they do. I see those fake mountains in the background or hear Nelson Eddy sing "Give me some men who are stout-hearted men," and I just cry and cry. It's not sadness. It feels like a release of something. Something I have been holding onto for many years. You know I can't stand emotion. I simply can't take it. I am not strong enough to take it. But lately all I do is cry about things that are not even sad. And another thing. I sing. I walk down the street singing. I sing in the subway while I am waiting for the train to come. I know people look at me and think I'm weird, but I sing, "Sweetheart! Sweetheart! Sweetheart!" But it's strange. The weeping and the singing—they make me feel more like myself—like the person I was before John died all those years ago.

When I explored with Bianca why she thought Nelson Eddy and Jeanette MacDonald had freed something in her, she said, "You know, my mother used to love them. She used to take me to their movies when I was a child. And she listened to operettas on the radio when she was at home. She would sing along, and she would bounce me on her knee and encourage me to sing too."

Bianca often expressed the idea that she is losing her "tether" to the world. Devoted to her Catholicism and horrified by the war in Iraq and the vulgarity of popular culture, she said, "The world is getting stranger and stranger to me. I feel more and more like I have no place in it. But when I watch Nelson Eddy and Jeanette MacDonald, I feel like the old world I knew, the world where your mother told you what was right and wrong, so that you knew by six or seven how to be a moral person—I feel like I haven't lost that world—like I can have it back for the asking." Bianca seemed to be regressing in a therapeutic way to her happy childhood days with her musical mother, and her identification with that singing mother, had allowed Bianca to sing and finally weep and feel more like her true self.

The Case of Winifred

A woman I will call Winifred is ninety-four and terribly infirm. She is confined to a wheelchair, wears diapers, and, though she has relatively good mental functioning, is forgetful and childlike. Freud would certainly say that for this woman, life is over. And yet, something that I find fascinating is going on with her. Winifred has the good fortune to still be in her own home, where she is taken care of by a devoted daughter with the assistance of another woman named Bridget who cooks and helps the daughter with Winifred's care.

Winifred has told me about her childhood. She was the fifth of six daughters. Her mother had no time to mother her. Her father favored two of Winifred's older sisters and adored Winifred's younger sister, the baby of the family. Winifred told me, "My father called my older sisters Princess and Precious. He called me Pill." She chuckled, "I guess I was an angry little girl, and he didn't like it." Winifred felt that she had become an alcoholic as an adult because of the anger she had tried to repress with her drinking.

Now, her daughter allowed her two small glasses of wine every night and no more. After the second glass, Winifred would say meekly, "Could I please have some more?" He daughter would say, "No, honey. It's not good for you. It's time to eat dinner, and then you have to go to bed." Winifred would nod submissively. She told me, "Bridget cooks for me, just for me. She makes chicken and dumplings, my favorite, just for me!"

Winifred is very ill and her illness causes her a lot of suffering. She is also rather lonely. She told me, "All my friends are dead." I have sometimes wondered what keeps Winifred alive, what keeps her going. But lately when I have come to visit her, I see the pleasure she takes in being wheeled around in her wheelchair, like a baby in a stroller. I observe how she gets enjoyment from being bathed and dressed by the two kind women who care for her. Winifred is, at long last, being babied. She is finally the only child and because of this, despite her near senility, something important is being healed in her.

Old age then provides another opportunity to work through the issues of infancy and the relationship to the pre-Oedipal mother. I have been told that the last word uttered by fatally wounded men in foxholes and by the elderly dying in hospice is "Mama." Given the enormous power of and cathexis to the woman who gave us birth throughout our lives, is it any wonder that we have had to perceive woman as organless and castrated?

CHAPTER FOUR

What Does Woman Want? A New Perspective

Sigmund Freud was baffled by women all his life. Though he spent many years exploring and charting what he called the "dark continent" (1926, 212) of female sexuality, he felt uneasy about the map he provided until the end of his life. In 1928, he told Ernest Jones, "everything we know of feminine early development appears to me unsatisfactory and uncertain" (Gay 1988, 501). As late as 1932, Freud admitted that his theories of femininity were "certainly incomplete and fragmentary" and he advised his reader that, should she wish to know more about the female sex, she ought to "consult your own life's experience or turn to the poets, or wait until science can give you deeper and more coherent information (Freud 1932, 135). At about the same time, Freud wrote to his friend Marie Bonaparte, complaining that he had been doing research into the "feminine soul" for thirty years with little to show for it. He asked, "*Was will das Weib?*"—"What does Woman want?" (Gay 1988, 501).

Freud was surrounded by powerful women all his life. He was profoundly influenced by his beautiful, strong-willed, and adoring mother, Amalia. The great passion of his life was his wife, Martha Bernays; her sister, Minna, became a valued companion (and some say, lover) with whom he could think out loud about his psychoanalytic theories. His daughter Anna had a formidable intellect, and in a way that none of Freud's sons was able to do, she became his heir. Radical for his time, Freud admitted female analysts such as Helene Deutsch, Karen Horney, and Jeanne Lampl-de Groot into his inner circle and welcomed their contributions (Gay 1988). Indeed, Freud's whole body of work can be seen as a progression from a masculine, nineteenth-century worldview, based on science and rational logic, to a more feminine and modern perspective that is broad enough to include the importance of intuition and the unconscious (Breger 1981). Freud's progression from science to art was never completed, leaving psychoanalysis and its followers with an often contradictory and value-laden theory; nowhere is this more evident than in his thinking about feminine psychology.

Many writers have speculated on how Freud's particular psychology influenced his theories about women. Atwood and Stolorow (1999) described how the defenses that Freud employed to protect his idealized vision of his mother from his deeply unconscious ambivalence and anger toward her had a profound effect on his psychosexual theories. In particular, sources of evil (such as the death instinct) were internalized, hostility was displaced onto the father, and the split-off, devalued maternal image was relegated solely to the psychology of the little girl. Hoffman (1996, 38) wrote that Freud's theories about women were consistently based on the adolescent conception that women's passions are dangerous and need to be controlled. Woman's aggression has to be denied and avoided by the man, who might doubt her capacity to sublimate it, and by the woman herself, who is frightened of retribution if she is too active or aggressive.

The fear of engulfment by a powerful mother, which is a crucial factor in human development for both boys and girls, is a dynamic that Freud almost totally ignored, perhaps because, as all analysts know, the most difficult case to analyze is our own. Ultimately, however, all such interpretations seem glib and irrelevant in light of the significant body of theory Freud did contribute to our knowledge of female development. The concepts of penis envy, the Oedipus complex, anatomy as destiny, the importance of the pre-Oedipal period for girls, and the idea, only touched on by Freud, that pregnancy is a developmental milestone in a woman's life, are all astonishingly fresh and crucial to an understanding of female development.

It is Freud's blind spot about women, related to the fear of maternal engulfment, which I believe is the key to an answer to his question, "What does woman want?" Men and women create different responses to the virtually universal fear of maternal engulfment. Though both sexes find solutions to the problem of separating from their first object, the female solution creates psychic constellations that can leave the adult woman with deep hungers, mysterious longings, and persistent discontents. Women indeed *want* profoundly, and often what they desire most is unconscious to them. Freud can be forgiven for being baffled, since, in truth, most women are themselves confused about what they want, why they feel "empty," or angry at what they most want to please. The magnitude of feminine desire, even greed, which Freud intuited with his question, is a danger that makes woman threatening, not only to men but also to herself.

The internal triangle of maternal imago, paternal imago, and self is set up in the female unconscious as a solution to the problem of separating from the mother with whom the girl has to identify and gaining mastery over the frustrating object of the father. It's an elegant solution to a uniquely feminine dilemma, and it is responsible for the intuition and empathy that is associated with femininity; but these feminine gifts come at a high price, because the internal triangle also gives new meaning to the idea that "three's a crowd." Since both the maternal and paternal introjects have powers that the little girl doesn't possess, the female ego is almost always bullied by its own introjects, and this encourages the submission, passivity, and masochism that are associated with the truly "feminine" woman. This intrapsychic dynamic is implicated in the almost universal subordination of women that anthropologists and sociologists describe.

Some feminists have argued that the earliest societies were matriarchal in character; that is, that women dominated these primitive cultures by virtue of their godlike procreativity. As long as human beings were ignorant about the role taken by men in the reproduction of the species, they argue, it is likely that fertility and maternity were revered as sacred functions, and that family lineage was organized around women. Unfortunately, most sociologists believe that there is no real evidence that woman-centered societies ever existed (Rosaldo and Lamphere 1974). Whether they did or not, it is important to consider that the oppression of women is reborn in the primitive unconscious of every human being long before culture ever has a chance to affirm it. The superiority of the penis is set down in the unconscious of both boys and girls so early and so deeply that it makes all later cultural subordination of women feel "natural." The internal triangle—though it solves the problem of separating from while still identifying with an object—also sets the stage for the female ego to be totally dominated by its own identifications. The feminist movement has labored gallantly to right the wrongs of patriarchal culture, but it is important for anyone interested in women's rights to understand how deep the roots of sexism really are. The reproduction of the social organization of gender occurs through transformations in the unconscious of each human being, long before it is reflected in cultural institutions. Psychoanalysis, so long perceived by feminists as "antiwoman," has an invaluable blueprint that can explain why sexual inequality gets reinvented again and again within the psyche of each new human being, so that the domination of women feels inevitable to both sexes.

The subjugation that women experience from *within* is infinitely more insidious than their subordination to a masculine culture. Because the intrapsychic coercion is largely unconscious and established at a time when the female ego is still young and fragile, women cannot deal with this oppression in a realistic manner. Without the benefit of psychoanalysis, most women don't even experience this subjugation consciously. Instead, it can manifest itself as inexplicable mood swings, psychological exhaustion, nameless longings, and irrational angers. Ask such a woman what she wants and she becomes inarticulate and teary, a mystery even to herself.

Clinical Examples

How does this oppression express itself clinically? What does it actually sound like? Jessica came to her session one day, guilty because she had had a fight with her boyfriend, which she herself didn't understand:

> His father and mother came into town from California and wanted to take him to the Four Seasons. I had to work that night. He asked me if I wanted to go, but I knew he was nervous about seeing them and wasn't really up to introducing me to them yet, so I told him I had to work. But the next day he called me and was going on and on about how great it all was, and I just blew up and told him he never thinks about my feelings. I've never even been to the Four Seasons. He said to me, "But I asked you to go!" And I said, "But I know you didn't really want me." And he said, "I don't understand women," and I didn't know what to say, because he did ask me after all.

I asked Jessica what prevented her from accepting her boyfriend's initial invitation. She said, "I knew he really didn't want me to go." I said, "What about what you want?" She said, "I can't be comfortable if he's uncomfortable. I just wanted him to want me."

Jessica's explanation of this situation seemed to indicate that her understanding of her boyfriend's feeling that she might be an intrusion took precedence over her own desires. Allying herself with his ambivalence, she became an impediment in his reunion with his parents. Her wish to meet her boyfriend's parents and eat at the Four Seasons was intrapsychically shouted down by her compulsive identification with his feelings.

Amy, an Asian American woman, was a highly successful investment banker on Wall Street. She came to treatment because "my biological clock is ticking." Never married, she was approaching forty, and she realized that delaying a decision about having a child was fast becoming a decision not to ever mother. In treatment, Amy spoke with scorn about her own mother:

> She's one of those Chinese lotus blossoms, purely decorative. The only thing she's ever been successful at is sex and pleasing a man. She has my father wrapped around her little finger, and it's totally disgusting. She cooks for him, dresses in the old-fashioned Chinese way for him. I'm surprised she doesn't bind her feet. I would really think she was stupid if I didn't understand how manipulative she is. She treats her children as notches on her gun. If I went to Yale, and my brother is a doctor, she's a successful woman. Never mind that she was a terrible mother and never accomplished anything professionally.

As treatment progressed, it became clear that Amy's resistance to finding a husband and having a child was based on her conviction that she had no choice but to duplicate her mother's experience. She said, "I'm going to have to divorce my mother if I'm ever going to get married and have a baby." Later, she admitted that she secretly longed to have her mother's sexual powers:

> My father loves my mother unconditionally. He doesn't care about his kids. He only has eyes for her. He thinks she hung the moon. No one has ever loved me like that. No one has ever bought me beautiful clothes and paid for my vacations. I guess I'm too independent. Sometimes I get tired of working twenty-four/seven and just want a man to take care of me.

Amy, though seemingly independent and separate from her mother, was unconsciously oppressed by her. Her "mother-in-me" had so much psychic power that Amy was not free to fantasize herself as any other kind of mother than the one she had. The goal of treatment soon became to free Amy from her subordination to the maternal imago, so that her ego could decide how she wanted to be like her mother and how she wanted to be different.

Jennifer, a woman going through her third divorce, came to treatment to try to understand her own passivity. Born wealthy, she found herself at the age of fifty in a bleak financial situation. Her three husbands had gone through her inheritance in a dismal progression of unemployment, excessive spending, and bad business decisions. She said, "Larry always rented these grand apartments for a king's ransom, and then he would spend several hundred thousand dollars fixing them up. I thought it was foolish to spend so much on decorating a rental. I always wanted us to own our own apartment, but Larry thought New York real estate was a bad investment." I asked what she thought about that, and she looked blank for a moment and replied, "Well, I understood how he felt." I said, "I know you did, but that's not what

I asked you. I asked if you think New York real estate is a bad investment." Though she had just said that she had always wanted to own her own apartment, Jennifer was stymied. After a moment, she said, "I don't understand what you mean. Larry is a businessman." It would be many months before Jennifer made a connection between her three husbands and her controlling, manic-depressive father—and many more before she began to be able to separate her thoughts and feelings from those of the men in her life.

Francis, who had been in analysis for many years, took her new boyfriend to her childhood home in Nantucket. She came back from vacation with the following story.

> There are two ways to get to the beach from my house. You can walk along the beach or along the road. For thirty-five years, I have been walking along the beach. But Doug wanted to walk along the road. So we did. But what was so interesting is what happened in my mind. I began to think that I had been crazy to ever think that walking along the beach was a good idea. After all, the road was shady. You didn't get sand between your toes. But while I was thinking all this, I noticed that I was really getting annoyed at Doug. And I thought, "Why? What has he done?" And I realized that he hadn't done anything to me. All he had done was say, "Let's walk along the road." I did the rest. I squelched myself. So I said, "Doug, I like to walk along the beach, so how about if we walk along the road to the beach and walk along the beach back to the house?" And you know what he said? He said, "Sure!" Isn't that amazing!

Francis, after working hard in analysis, was able to use her strengthened ego to observe the intrapsychic compulsion to subordinate herself to the internalized Oedipal father. Once she understood the conflict, she was able to resolve the situation in a way that utilized both her ability to empathize and her own feelings.

The Case of Elise

Elise was a physical therapist and dancer who came to individual and group treatment because she was concerned about "a deep sadness in me that's just there all the time." Delicate and ethereal, Elise had struggled with anorexia most of her life. She embraced the role of "healer" and more than anyone in the group, she wanted to be helpful to others. Yet she hated the tendency among the women in the group to see themselves as victims. She would always ask, "Well, what part of you needed to attract an alcoholic? What part of yourself was he expressing?" Her own life was not immune to this kind of thinking. Though her ex-husband, a successful actor, had left her because he had fallen in love with her best friend, Elise was trying to explore what she had unconsciously been expressing by "setting this up." What lesson was she trying to teach herself by "drawing this energy" toward herself?

Elise was involved with a man who was bisexual. Greg was addicted to cocaine and, when he took drugs, he went on homosexual binges. As his drug habit intensified, he found himself in deep debt, and Elise reported several frightening encounters with drug dealers who were owed money. When Greg confessed to having unprotected sex in gay bars, Elise wept, but defended Greg against the group's attacks, saying, "He's open to the world. He won't be bound by other people's prudishness." The other group members felt more and more apprehensive as Elise decided to invite her lover to live with her and her three children. She also reported that, though she was fifty-two, she was trying to have another baby. Group members expressed anger at Elise for her "lack of responsibility." They told Elise that they thought she was putting her family and herself in danger. But Elise did not feel frightened. She felt excited by the "freedom to misbehave" that Greg permitted himself, and she felt that she had brought him into her life, because he acted out an aspect of her character with which she needed to be comfortable.

A few weeks later, Elise told the group the following story. Greg had come to her apartment and shown Elise and her teenage son nude pictures of an old girlfriend. Though she was again fighting tears, Elise had a brave smile on her face. She said,

> Greg knew that it would make my son feel so grown up to look at pictures of a naked woman. It was so cute the way they elbowed each other and talked about "what a great ass" she had. I mean, why are we so squeamish in this society? We admire beautiful paintings and beautiful buildings and beautiful minds. Why not a beautiful ass? Why can't it be admired logically and objectively? Greg wants to see an open world where there's no such thing as "boy talk" and "girl talk." If he can go to the museum with me, why can't I go to the porn shop with him and enjoy it?

Elise couldn't understand why this incident had "touched such a sad place in me. I'm so moralistic and prudish. I don't know what's wrong with me." The other members of the group assured her there was nothing wrong with her; what Greg had done was very hurtful. They couldn't understand why Elise wasn't furious. I said, "This group doesn't understand. Elise is so good at identifying with Greg's position that she has no energy left to know what's she's feeling toward him."

Elise reported that her children disliked Greg intensely and would lock themselves in their rooms when he was in the apartment. She said,

> I think I use my children to create a boundary around me. They express my negative feelings about Greg so that I don't have to. I tell him he can't come over because it would upset my daughter, Michele, but the truth is I need to carve out some space for myself. When everyone is in the house together, I'm just exhausted with ambivalence. I feel hurt at the way the children treat him, and yet I want him to just get the hell out and leave us all alone.

I asked Elise, "Whose feelings are these?" She said, "They're mine." Other group members disagreed, pointing out that Greg's hurt and her children's rage had crowded out Elise's ability to know what she herself was feeling.

The next week, Elise reported that she was disturbed by the anger she had been experiencing. She said, "I love my children, but I just want them to go away. They exhaust me. All that noise and exuberance. I lose myself in it. I can't access myself when they're around. I realized this week that that's why I smoke. I love to draw the smoke into my lungs. I can feel the space it makes, and I think, 'This is my space. No one else can get to it.' I don't have energy to do anything. All I want to do is close the bathroom door and soak in the tub. I told Greg I didn't want to see him anymore."

Elise told the group in the next session that she "had a hard week." The teacher of her poetry class had criticized Elise's poems about her childhood. She said that the instructor had said, "This is a fairy tale. Get real, Elise. What did your mother do to you?" Elise said, through tears, "I feel like everything I have structured my life on fell apart in that moment. I can't do that. I don't know how to do that." I asked, "Do what?" Elise said,

> Attack my mother. I can't attack my mother. It's like attacking myself. It's like we're one person. I don't know where I end, and she begins. It's like she's inside me. I was always the one who supported my mother. And she supported me. She needed me to be happy. She used to pretend that everything was fine, was wonderful. She used to say, "you are such a lucky, lucky child." But all her pleasures brought her pain. She loved to garden and arrange flowers, but she tortured herself doing it. She just worked and worked because everything had to be perfect. She won awards, but she was torturing herself. She used to wash dishes without gloves, and her hands were blistered and cracked, and she loved it. She loved pain. She used to stand at the kitchen sink on one leg like a Zen warrior until her supporting leg was blue. She was weeping psychically. She was always cutting her fingers and burning herself in the kitchen. It was a form of self-mutilation. Eating was torture. Every bite she put in her mouth, she talked

> about how fattening it was. I mean, we had some serious anorexic issues here. And I'm like her, and I've trained my daughter to be like her. Michele is anorexic too. Even the things I enjoy, my ballet dancing—I do it till I'm abusing myself, like my mother.

Another woman in the group, Lynn, said, "You're not like your mother. I hate your mother!" Elise put her hands in front of her face and said,

> No, no, no! I can't be angry at my mother! It's so unfair. She was abused by my father all her life, and she did the best she could. My ability to empathize with her and take away her pain is terribly important. My anger would hurt her. How could I? There she was standing on one leg. She would have collapsed if I had been mad at her.

I said, "That was then. What about now, here in this group? If you were angry at her here, would that obliterate the love you feel toward her?" Elise said, "She just seems too delicate. She needs protection." I said, "I'll protect her. You say everything you need to say, and I'll protect your mother. You can give her to me to protect awhile." Elise laughed, though she was still crying, and she said, "Thank you. Thank you for that. I believe you could do it."

Elise told the group that she had had a very strict and sadistic nanny from the time she was born who "denied me access to my mother." The nanny told Elise that if she cried and upset her mother, her mother would decide that she was "crazy" and take Elise to the doctor for an injection. This terrified the young girl. Though Elise was afraid of the dark, the nanny insisted she sleep without a night-light and she would lock Elise's door, so that she couldn't get up and look for her mother. Elise said, "I was always trying to hide from nanny and find my mother, but she was always in another part of the house. I couldn't get to her." To comfort herself, Elise had an enormous collection of teddy bears—"So many there was hardly room for me in the bed"—and she mothered them all when she couldn't sleep. The nanny left when Elise was nine, and after that, Elise became her mother's "comfort. We lived next door to a graveyard, and I used to ride my bicycle through there and gather flowers from the newly dug graves. I took them home to my mother to alleviate her pain."

After these disclosures, Elise reported feeling "freer in a strange way." But she also said that she felt "starved" after group was over and she went home. She said, "I can't hold the group in my mind during the week. I feel very nurtured here, but I lose it as soon as I leave." Elise guiltily told the group that Greg was back in her life. Several of the women were outraged at this news but Elise defended her lover.

> I need him, because he gives me the feeling that he loves me just as I am, unconditionally. He's just for me. If I were a total failure, if I were a drug addict, he would still love me. I want to love him the way he loves me, unconditionally. I want to give him that gift.

"But, Elise," Lynn said, "*Greg* is the drug addict, not you. Greg is the failure. And I think you struggle to love him unconditionally, because that is the way you want to be loved, not for your ability to understand and take care of people. Just for yourself. I feel I love you that way. Why can't this group give you the unconditional acceptance you need, so that you can get rid of Greg? I tell you I love you but somehow it's just words to you."

I said, "It's hard to feed a starving person." Elise said,

> You just said something profound, Lucy. I remember when my daughter was so terribly anorexic. When Michele was sick, I was sick too, and we used to lie in bed together, and I would try to feed her. It would take hours to get her to eat one tiny shrimp. She was starving, but she couldn't be fed. And I couldn't eat either. I am a prisoner of my own identifications, but what can I do?

Lynn said, "Lucy, I want you to try to feed Elise a shrimp." I asked what I should say. Lynn said, "Something to free her from the prison she's talking about." I said, "Elise is a genius at feeling other people's feelings. Her intuition is a great gift, but it also imprisons her." I told Elise to watch how she always knows and feels and understands what everyone is feeling, but that she is usually not aware of what she feels toward them. "This is the lifeline out of prison," I said, "to know what you feel toward others, not with others."

Elise said, "I guess I'm a little annoyed at my children."

The next week, Elise talked about her father. Though she had always described him as "abusive" to her mother, Elise now said,

> There was something so sad about him, so very sad. There was a gentleness and a vulnerability that he had to hide in the WASPy environment he grew up in. He was a bookish person in a world where men were valued for how well they could play tennis. He never hit my mother. His abuse was much more elegant than that. He used to humiliate her at the dinner table in this very subtle way. I knew he did it because he was so unhappy, so isolated. Criticizing my mother was the only form of misbehavior he allowed himself. I used to go into his study after dinner and try to distract him from his book and make him laugh. And I could do it. I was the only one who could make him laugh. Because I understood his sorrow. On the nights when he actually kissed me good night, I was euphoric. We never touched in my family. That's why all these words mean

> nothing to me. I grew up with words, words, words, but they were all empty, and no one touched anyone else. I was hungry for touch.

After this, Elise was extremely ambivalent about Greg. She wanted to end the relationship because she was beginning to realize that "he's just not a successful person." She would ask him not to call her, but when he would appear at her door, she always relented. She reported the following dream:

> I was in a big room with all the important men in my life. My husband, my father, Greg, and some man I didn't recognize, a mystery man, were all there. They were all falling apart. They were either psychotic or drunk. I was scared. I realized I couldn't depend on any of them for the qualities I need from them. My husband wasn't going to provide financial stability, and Greg wasn't going to give me unconditional love and acceptance. I realized I was going to have to provide what I need for myself. I was terrified. I turned around, and I saw you, Lucy, and I thought, "Oh, Lucy will help me get control of this situation."

Despite her apparent feeling that I could be an ally in getting control of these undependable men, Elise continued to see Greg. When the group challenged her about it, she said:

> I don't know how to get someone out of my life. I just can't do it. I can't reject him. How do you tell a person, "You're just not enough"? I think because I have felt so rejected in my life, so unimportant to my parents, that I just can't imagine giving someone that I've loved that feeling. I feel like it would break my heart more than his.

Discussion

Elise's empathy, potentially a great gift, is not in the service of her ego. The "deep sadness that's just there all the time" expresses the oppression of her ego because of her compulsive identification with the significant objects in her life. Her attempts to heal and understand the adulterer, the drug addict, her anorexic mother, and her cold father can all be understood as attempts to heal herself. How was this dynamic laid down in her character and how does it serve the discharge of her drives in the "here and now" of the group?

Meadow (2000) reflected on the earliest longings of the preverbal patient relating to a dyad, and not the triad, of the Oedipal period. When the preverbal child is fed, she may create a blissful fantasy of a union with a wonderful internal cause of her pleasure often experienced as the patient's own omnipotence (15). This euphoric experience of an internal force that reduces drive tension is structuring to the ego. Indeed, it is crucial to the development of a sense of self. The search for union with another person, in this case the mother that Elise could never find, can be seen as a longing for a missing part of the self. Because Elise was "denied access" to her mother, and most probably lacked this structuring feeling of internal omnipotence, the stage was set preverbally for her ego to be oppressed by the later internalization of the maternal and paternal imagoes. Elise's anorexia can then be considered as a somatic expression of the longing to feel whole and satiated in an atmosphere of deprivation. It says: I can be in control and autonomous by not being fed.

Foxe (1995) discussed how this preverbal failure to achieve a strong sense of self and autonomy can keep some women's selves inescapably bound to the mother where they remain attuned only to her feelings (143). In describing the dynamics underlying the anorectic character, Foxe talked about the danger of receiving sustenance, whether actual or symbolic food, as the sense of guilt attached to being "entitled to life," which is each child's struggle to individuate and separate internally from the primary object. Having something for oneself means depriving the primary object, perhaps fatally (134).

As the object world began to form in Elise's mind, she created a psychic solution to her mother's absence. She internalized the maternal imago and began to feel the closeness she desired from her mother by feeling her mother's feelings. This "mother-in-me" had advantages for Elise. Because she could empathize with and soothe her mother, she was "the most important child" in the family. Such a longing for importance expresses the missing preverbal experience of omnipotence that Meadow describes. The identification with mother also protected Elise from the aggressive impulses which she experienced as so dangerous to her fragile mother.

Becoming the mother of teddy bears, Elise was able to comfort herself. This aping of motherly activity represented not only a longing for but also a warding off of the nurturing object. Spotnitz and Meadow (1976) framed identification as useful as a defense against aggression. They remind us that the ability to identify requires less cathexis than does loving, in that all that identification requires is the perception in the mind's object field of an autoplastic representation which can then be viewed as part of the self (58). The protection of the internalized object image, though it defends against aggressive impulses, requires the sacrifice of self (51), rendering Elise's ego as fragile as her physical person.

Though Elise cannot attack her mother because it would be an attack on herself, she does struggle with unconscious aggression toward her maternal object. Bringing flowers from the graves of the dead to her mother can certainly be understood as a murderous wish. More important, the identification with her cold, critical father expresses her aggressive impulses toward her mother.

The choice of Greg as object is useful to Elise on several levels. He gives her the "unconditional love" that was missed in the first relationship with mother. Identifying with him allows her to repeat the experience with her mother, this time in the role of the powerful parent. Because Greg, like her, has been so rejected, she can express this personal longing for unconditional love by refusing to reject him, no matter what. His "freedom to misbehave" serves to heal the oppressed and repressed internalized father whose only form of misbehavior was an attack on the mother. It also expresses Elise's wish to assert herself in misbehavior.

Bollas (1987) described the way each person transfers elements of the parent's child care to his own handling of himself as an object. We establish a sense of "twoness" through the internalization of the process of being the other's object (59). Elise's self-perception, handling, and, above all, her self-refusal express her internalized parental process still engaged in handling the self as an object. The neglectful maternal imago and the critical, distant paternal imago continue to attack Elise's ego, so that all she can present clinically is a deep sadness overlaid with a compulsive, almost manic tendency to identify with and understand everyone in the object world.

In the group, Elise protects herself from her own aggressive impulses by consistently identifying with everyone. This identification exhausts all libidinal energy, leaving nothing but a deep sadness and an inability to experience true object love and savor life.

Elise talks frequently about boundaries around her and a wish for a sense of "space" that belongs to her and cannot be intruded upon by her identifications. Often, she has equated boundaries with negative feelings. She would like to be able to "lock all her doors" and find herself. But when I try to encourage her to find a feeling *toward* rather than *with* another, she is stymied. No matter how much other group members may monopolize with depressive talk or manipulate with neediness or attack out of anxiety and fear, Elise will only respond, "Well, of course, I understand how she feels, and I just feel so sorry . . ."

Lately, Elise has seemed to relax the compulsively cheerful demeanor and manicky optimism that she uses to ward others off. The butterfly has landed and settled into the sadness, which, for now, is the truest expression of her sense of self available to her.

Getting What She Wants

Bollas (1987, 62) said that the creation of a space for the holding of the self as an object of one's nurture is an essential contribution that clinical psychoanalysis can make to the patient. But if the internal triangle is characterized by a rather impoverished ego being tyrannized by two toxic parental imagoes, it becomes difficult or impossible to access the space required for the nurturance and feeding of the self. How then can an analyst work with the oppressively "feminine" woman to help her carve out such a space?

The neutral environment of the individual psychoanalytic session can be maturational to these patients. The analyst who limits herself to three to five object-oriented questions in the hour and resists the temptation to overstimulate with interventions is providing the patient an expansive arena for the fragile ego to develop. The discipline of silence is particularly difficult with these women, because they want the analyst to talk. They invite the therapist to intrude herself on the analysis, because it makes it easier to then "identify" with the analyst. Compulsive identification with the object in the here and now protects the patient from the grief and rage that are the truest expressions of the impoverished self.

Though these empathic women often induce anger in the analyst toward the internalized objects, it is usually not helpful to express this feeling to the patient, even if it feels like joining or protecting the patient from oppression from within. An attack by the analyst on the parental imago usually serves to strengthen the identificatory defense, thereby reinforcing the subjection of the ego. Rather, it is more helpful for the analyst to symbolically offer herself as a holding environment for the protection of the parental imago, while the patient goes about the business of saying everything.

The interplay of projection and introjection in the session is particularly important with patients like Elise. Projecting the internalized object onto the analyst sets the stage for feelings *toward*, not *with*, the parental imago. Likewise, the projection of this imago *into* the analyst for "protection" frees the budding ego to emerge. By recognizing and accepting these projections, the analyst can help the patient approach the object playfully, molding and shaping it into a more elastic, less rigid imago. The articulation and transformation of this now-externalized object is the primary work of analysis, and the goal becomes the reintegration of the object into the self, where it can be used by the ego to enhance relationships in the world. Margolis (1994, 230) wrote that progress in analysis—with its structuring consolidation of boundaries between the self and others—can be measured by observing an increased capacity in the patient for assertive verbal communication.

What does woman want? She wants to be able to use her empathy and intuition in the service of her own ego. She wants the feminine tendency to identify to be a tool, not a prison. She wants to be liberated from the oppression of the internal triangle and be able to encounter her internalized objects playfully, not compulsively. The longing implied in Freud's original question, "What does woman want?" expresses an important idea and it is this: Life becomes complex, rich, and meaningful only when we can experience and savor both self and other.

CHAPTER FIVE

~

Women in Groups and Women's Groups

Women in groups, like women in life, often tend to play the role of the "second sex" (de Beauvoir 1952), that is, they subtly subvert themselves to the men around them. This dynamic is largely unconscious to both men and women and both sexes play a part in creating it. It manifests itself in a multitude of complex patterns of *man as subject* and *woman as object*. It can be quite blatant, as when men do all of the talking and talk only to other men, while the women sit silently; but often, it is expressed in a more elegantly intricate fashion. The clinician will find herself with a group where the men have "problems" and the women energetically attempt to "solve" them. In other groups, the men will talk about their lives, and the women will "identify" with them. In situations like these, women may be getting so much appreciation for their empathy and their insight that it is almost impossible to spot the fact that the focus is firmly masculine.

The most skilled group leader, whether male or female, may overlook this tendency, since all men and women, because of the vicissitudes of becoming masculine and feminine, see this situation as "second nature." A female therapist with a feminist perspective may rush to see the men in her group as "oppressors" and the women as "victims," but if she does, she will be oversimplifying what is happening in a way that can be destructive to group members of both sexes. To resolve this sexist resistance and promote progressive communication between men and women, it is important for the clinician to consider how this dynamic develops in the unconscious of all people.

The domination of women is set up in the preverbal development of both sexes because of the universal fact that girls have a biological mother of the same sex while boys do not. While both males and females begin life in narcissistic oneness with a woman, boys must achieve their masculine identity through an almost violent dis-identification with their mothers. The boy's penis clearly demonstrates that he is different from mother, and this gives him a path out of symbiosis that is not open to girls. He can identify with his father to deny the power of the mother and to obliterate the identification he has made with the female object in the pre-Oedipal period. His ability to identify with the mother is literally "smashed to pieces" (Freud 1925), and henceforth any empathy with a female point of view will likely be laced with anxiety about a regression to primitive symbiosis.

Little girls, with no penis to oppose the omnipotent mother, have a longer and more intense pre-Oedipal period. Mothers can more clearly see their sons as objects, while daughters are experienced as part of self, and this sets up a tendency in women toward boundary confusion. Women struggle with issues of separation and individuation and feelings of primary identification and love unmitigated by the reality principle throughout life (Chodorow 1978).

The internal triangle of maternal and paternal introjects and self, which is characteristic of the female psyche, allows women to use identification to solve a particularly unique female problem, the challenge of separating from the maternal object while still retaining a feminine identity. With no penis to oppose engulfment by the omnipotent pre-Oedipal mother, girls attempt to gain control by introjection of the parental imagoes. Girls incorporate the pre-Oedipal mother with the ingestion of her milk; this "mother-in-me" is never destroyed, as it is in boys. Instead, the feminine endopsychic world is rendered more complex at the end of the Oedipal period, when little girls resolve the conflicts of that difficult stage by introjecting the paternal imago as well.

Though the internal triangle provides women with an enormous capacity for identification with both men and women, a rich imagination and intuition, and an ability to sacrifice the self for others, it is important to remember that it sets up other challenges for women. The triangle is often not equilateral and, unconsciously, the self takes a subordinate position in relation to the powerful maternal and paternal imagoes. When the girl introjects her Oedipal father, it is not the primitive incorporation that was characteristic of the earliest maternal identification. This time, the girl introjects not only the imago of the object but also the attitudes of that object and her relationship to it. Because of the challenges of his own development, the Oedipal father often has an unconscious wish to attack and dominate the powerful pre-Oedipal mother. This means that when the Oedipal girl introjects the father, she begins to identify with his wish to dominate and attack the maternal imago. This identification with dominating man gives her the pleasure of vicarious power over the pre-Oedipal mother within, but at the expense of her primary feminine identification. This intrapsychic process conditions women to submission, passivity, and a compulsive, unreciprocated empathy that borders on the masochistic (Holmes 2000).

Given the very real potential of this problem, it is easy to understand why many group leaders advocate women's groups. The argument explains that if men gain their identity by devaluing and denying any feminine identification within themselves, and if women compulsively lose themselves in identification and empathy, then it is a particularly challenging in a heterosexual group for women to be perceived by either sex as independent and autonomous subjects. Only in a single-gender group—where there are no anxious men to unconsciously subjugate and no opportunities for women to compulsively play handmaiden—can females be free to explore the integrity rather than the "otherness" of their issues.

Having run all-female groups for many years, I can attest to the fact that they can be highly effective, particularly for a certain type of "feminine" woman. These are women who, because of the difficulties of their own development, have become diffused in identifications. That is, the process of identification has become so compulsive that it is no longer in the service of the ego and it deprives the woman of the full possession of her own personality. These women are often subjugated by their unconscious identification with an oppressive paternal imago, which expresses itself in a masochistic dependence or a compulsive, self-destructive identification with the men in their lives.

The "Feminine" Woman in Group

Marilyn, a recently divorced woman, talked about the familiar sense of emptiness. She said, "I don't know who I am if I'm not married. It's not that I enjoyed marriage that much. I just desperately need to know that I'm Eric's wife, because if I'm not, then who am I?" Marilyn was frantic to find a boyfriend, because "if I had a boyfriend, I could feel okay about myself." Marilyn was addicted to diet and sleeping pills, and she recognized this as a problem, but she idolized her male doctor, seeing him as the ultimate authority about her health and her savior in her attempts to deal with her feelings of emptiness and despair. It seemed that Marilyn's sense of self was so weak that she was compelled to look everywhere for an idealized father in whom she could take refuge, even if that refuge meant the erosion of her own ego.

Jane was very clear that she wanted to be in a woman's group. She said she had things to say that couldn't be said in the presence of men. When I explored what those things might be, she said, "I don't know. I just talk differently when men are present. I have to be the ingénue, the perpetual little sweetheart. Men take up so much space, and their needs come first." Jane described an incident when she had delivered her son to the apartment of his father and the father's new girlfriend. She said, "My son started to cry. He didn't want to go in, so even though the girlfriend was there, I just took my son by the hand and marched in. I stayed until he was comfortable—you know, like a dog pees on everything to mark his territory and then moves on?" Jane blushed and giggled after she said this, and said, "Now that's something I never could have said if men were here!" When I asked why not, she said, "Men talk like that. Women are supposed to be ladylike." Despite his infidelity, Jane's husband moved back into her apartment every Christmas. Jane reported she put up with this, because "it makes the children happy. And family means so much to him." Though Jane complained that she could "never do my own work or see my friends over the holidays; it's all about him," it never occurred to her that her needs had any priority over those of her husband and children. She said, "I don't know how it happens, but I lose myself. All my doors, my refrigerator, even my bathroom door are open to all of them twenty-four hours a day." Her total identification with her family's feelings defended her from any aggression she might have felt toward them.

Jane described her new boyfriend to the group as "very loving and attentive, just for me." But she also said, "I totally immerse myself in his mind, his reality, and then I have to make myself some space so I can find myself again."

These feminine women were able to use an all-woman's group very effectively. With no masculine object present to compulsively play subject to, they seemed to carve out the time and the space they needed to begin to know themselves. Jane expressed the idea that "being in a group of women seems to slow me down, gives me the time to breathe so that I can find my own feelings." Marilyn compared the female group experience with going to the grocery store for the first time after Eric left her and their daughter went to college: "I stood in the aisle by the produce absolutely paralyzed, because I knew what my daughter likes to eat, and I knew what Eric likes to eat, but I didn't have a clue what I like to eat. I was so busy taking care of their needs that I had never taken the time to find out who I am, even what I like to eat. So I had to figure it out."

Evelyn had been in a mixed-gender group with a male analyst with whom she had been in constant conflict, and finally she left the group. Evelyn's individual analyst suggested that she might like to work with a female group analyst, and when I suggested a woman's group, she liked the idea. In the first session with her new group, Evelyn described her difficult relationship with the leader and the other men in her last group. She reported a dream in which the male group leader was "raping me from behind, and I had to pretend to enjoy it." Evelyn was somewhat "shamed" by this dream and was initially reluctant to talk about it. She said, "I'm a very sexual person," but she seemed to be embarrassed about it. A few weeks after joining the women's group, Evelyn reported another dream. She said, "It was sexual, like my dream of being raped, but this time I was riding a horse. I was in control, and it was very pleasurable." Evelyn told this dream with a sense of joy, and she made the association that this dream was about the new feelings of power she felt in the all-female group.

All these women had a rather impoverished sense of self, and in one form or another, they had all projected their oppressive internalized objects onto the people in their lives. In an all-women's group, each was able to begin to strengthen her own ego. Just as they did in life, all the women in group compulsively gave themselves away in identification with the other, and so the group resistance became an obsessive "helpfulness." They all rushed to empathize, support, and rescue each other, and any aggression or frustration that arose was masked by the group myth: "We are just alike and feel exactly the same feelings, and we are here to bolster each other up against an externalized enemy." This group resistance actually had a positive effect on the individual members for many months. Most of the women achieved a new awareness, mainly by seeing themselves in the mirror held up to them by the support and encouragement of other members. It took many more months before these women could risk talking about any negative feelings toward each other, and when the aggression did finally appear, it often expressed itself in unconscious identification with a parent, most often the mother.

The Case of Teresa

For example, Teresa, who had initially been very quiet, began to monopolize the group about her difficulties with her teenage son, who was physically abusing her. At first, the group, true to form, listened attentively and sympathetically. Teresa's tirade about her victimization at her son's hands was quite consonant with the group resistance that aggression, if it existed at all, resided outside the group. Everyone offered Teresa helpful suggestions, all of which fell on deaf ears as Teresa, in her distress, became more and more repetitive and obsessive. As the weeks went by, the group deteriorated into a private session for Teresa while the others sat in silence.

Louis R. Ormont talks about the moment when a group congeals, that is, the time when the group has gone from being emotionally chromatic to monochromatic. This difficult state of affairs is usually brought on by a shared reaction to a particular member (Ormont 1991, 66). I could see that the other women were getting increasingly frustrated and angry with Teresa, but they seemed unable to put their thoughts into words. When I asked Teresa why she thought everyone was so quiet, she said, "I have no idea," and went back to her monologue. I tried bridging (Ormont 1990), turning to Marilyn and asking her why she thought Susan was not saying anything. Marilyn said, "Well, I guess she doesn't know how to help." In desperation, I said, "Jane, what feeling does Teresa induce in you when she talks like this?" Jane looked flustered, paused, and said, "Well, I just understand how she feels, and I feel bad for her."

I began to think that Teresa would destroy the group. After several months of this, Teresa phoned between sessions to tell me another horror story about her son. I said, "Bring it up in group." Teresa started the next group by saying, "I called Lucy about a problem I'm having with my son, and she suggested I bring it up here." This finally was too much. Jane said,

> I can't believe this. How could you do that, Lucy? We've sat here for week after week, imprisoned by Teresa, while she talks and talks. None of us can say anything or influence her in any way. We just have to sit silently and endure it while she tortures us. And you told her to bring it up in group? Why didn't you tell her to come in for an individual session and torture you for a while?

I said, "Why should I have to deal with this alone? What's your resistance to helping me out a little?" Jane said, "I don't know what to do. You're the professional." I said, "Well, as a professional, I'm trying to understand why this group sits silently week after week while Teresa talks." At this point Teresa exclaimed, "Wait a minute! Lucy, you told me to bring this up. I don't monopolize. I'm just doing what you told me to do." Susan said, "What do you mean you don't monopolize? We sit here in a box you've put us in week after week, and we can't speak because none of our problems are as important as yours, and none of our suggestions are helpful. I feel like you've tied us all up and are holding us hostage to your misery."

At this point, Teresa began to cry. She said, "I just had a memory." I asked her what it was. She said,

> When I was a little girl, my mother had a very unusual way of punishing me if I had done something bad. She would make me stand in the middle of the kitchen floor while she berated me. She could do this for an hour or more. I had to stand very still and I wasn't allowed to say anything. I wasn't permitted to defend myself or apologize or disagree with her. I just had to stand there. Sometimes I had to go to the bathroom, but that didn't matter. I had to stand there until she was finished talking, till she was all worn out. And she could talk and talk and talk. I felt tied up and tortured.

Teresa's unconscious identification with her punishing mother allowed her to express anger in the group without ever being in touch with it. Until Jane's outburst, she had no idea that her monologue was enraging. She had used it to discharge aggression, while retaining her "feminine" identity as a gentle soul who was the victim of her male oppressor. Using her maternal imago to symbolically imprison, as her mother had imprisoned her, she was protected from her true feelings, which would have threatened her feminine identification.

Gradually, the group felt safer to express negative feelings not only toward me but also toward other members. And as they were more frank with Teresa, she was able to give up her obsessive monopolizing and tell us the emotionally significant story of her life. Even later, she felt secure enough to express the feelings that her monopoly had masked: "This group doesn't understand the depth of my suffering and has no power to protect me from the abuse of my son."

Ormont (1991, 75) writes, "An introject is a part object, a piece of some significant figure of the person's past, that remains incorporated in the psyche but has never been assimilated into the person's adult ego. It operates as a feeling, an attitude, a voice urging the person to act as the significant figure did. By implication, it urges others to act in the role of the patient himself." Teresa, in an unconscious identification with her maternal introject, had tortured the group as her mother tortured her. Once the group resistance and the congealing it produced had been resolved, the other women were freed to give Teresa back to herself; that is, they verbalized the anger she was unable to experience.

Women in a well-functioning group are able to move through and play with the internal objects in the rooms of the other members' minds. They shape their relationships in the room according to what Bollas (1992, 50) calls "the idiom of the internal world." Each woman can bring along the personal spirits or ghosts of her internal triangle and transfer them to a receptive place in another. When the group is functioning as a whole, and the leader is including all the members, the women are able to use both their compulsive need to identify and empathize and their aggression in highly effective ways. Identification provides a kaleidoscope of mirrors to each member, a multifaceted reflection of self that enriches each woman's understanding and acceptance of her own complexity. Aggression, used effectively, strengthens each member's sense of self against the oppressions of the endopsychic world of the feminine woman and frees her to use her empathy and identification, not in masochistic and compulsive ways, but in the service of her own ego.

Groups Organized around Female Developmental Milestones

Another situation in which women's groups are highly effective is when they are organized around the physical milestones of the female life cycle: the beginning of menstruation, pregnancy, and menopause. Though centered in the body, these dramatic developmental events set up crises in psychic functioning, periods of intense disequilibrium that can lead, in favorable circumstances, to maturation and the creation of new psychic structures. Body and mind are changing in ways that can be experienced as intensely traumatic. During these traumas, a woman's group can prove to be helpful. It is often difficult, if not impossible, for women to speak about such quintessentially feminine events in the presence of men. The stresses on women during these life crises may make the identification with and empathy for men, which allow communication between the sexes to flow smoothly, almost impossible. As one pregnant woman put it, "I literally have nothing to give men right now. All I can think about is my own body." Men, for their part, because of the fear of their own maternal engulfment, usually find a focus on these feminine issues irrelevant at best, and deeply threatening at worst. Women sense this and, in unconscious compliance or conscious embarrassment, stifle the impulse to speak about the issues that are most pressing in their lives. I recall a supervision group that contained five women and one man, all in their fifties. This group functioned very effectively and cooperatively in its presentation of patients until the day that the man was not able to attend the group. Spontaneously, the women began to talk about menopause, about everything from their anxieties about death to hot flashes and herbal remedies. At the end of the session, one of the female analysts said, "Well, I guess this was acting out in a major way, but I feel wonderful. I have absolutely nowhere to talk about any of this and I couldn't have talked about it here if Jeff had been here today!"

A Pregnancy Group

Lily, a woman who had recently discovered that she was pregnant with a much-wanted child, came into a group for pregnant women to discuss her mysterious "feelings of ambivalence." Her husband, Bob, was very excited about the impending birth but Lily was filled with uncertainty, dread, and fear. She was afraid she would "turn into my mother" when the baby was born, and she was anxious about the discomfort of pregnancy and the pain of childbirth. She had miscarried in her first pregnancy, and I encouraged her to verbalize all her negative feelings in the group, because I believed this would help her achieve her goal of holding on to this pregnancy. She said, "I can't talk to Bob about any of these fears. I get scared of making him resentful or angry. I think, in my gut, I'm scared to complain to a man. My father used to hit us if we complained, and he wasn't interested in my feelings." Oppressed by a harsh paternal introject that she had projected onto her husband, Lily had a lot of complaining to do, and she was able to use the pregnancy group very effectively to explore all the feelings her pregnancy induced. When she left the group after the birth of her son, she felt "much safer to be open with Bob about my feelings."

One of the most difficult feelings that pregnancy seems to induce in women is a primitive and seemingly unreasonable hatred and resentment toward their husbands and partners. Naomi, who had told me that she had a good marriage and loved her husband very much, said, "I don't know what it is, but since I've been pregnant, I feel differently. I don't want to look at him, I don't want to have sex with him, and I feel guilty to say it, but I usually just feel like I hate him." Martha, who had always loved her domestic role, said, "My husband is such a big baby. He expects me to take care of him like a mother, and I'm pregnant. I do the laundry, clean the house, and he's the one who complains about being tired. He doesn't know what tired is. I'd really like to kill him!"

If women don't express Martha's aggression toward her husband, they will often verbalize indifference in a rather aggressive way. Leona said, "My husband just can't understand my total lack of sexual interest in him right now. He just doesn't get it. It's not him. It's me. I think if Brad Pitt were standing naked in front of me, I would just want to take a nap."

Women often feel abandoned by the fathers of their babies during pregnancy. Polly said, "I feel so alone in this pregnancy. He's not really with me, and he's not being supportive. I think deep down, I'm afraid he's going to abandon me and the baby."

Pregnancy is often experienced in the unconscious as a frightening confrontation with the powerful pre-Oedipal mother of the internal triangle, and this confrontation is perceived as the fault of the man who impregnated her. A pregnant woman reported the following dream:

> I was lying in bed beside a mean and evil man. We were in a grand house, sort of like the house I grew up in. I knew I had to get away from the man, that he was dangerous. I ran down the stairs. The servants were helping me escape. I ran out the front door, thinking, "I'm really going to escape. He's not going to kill me after all!" A limousine was waiting for me, and the servants rushed me into the car. I looked back, and the evil man had come to the door, and he had a baby with him, and I thought, "Oh! I had forgotten there was a child! I can't leave the baby." Somehow the baby made the man less evil.

The house in this dream was associated with her childhood home and seems—like the frightening dream of bleeding which was somehow her husband's fault (see chapter 2, p. 33)—to express an association between houses and the early mother. The murderous man lies with her within this house/mother, and he wants to kill her. Though the forgotten baby makes him feel somewhat less evil, the dreamer still has a fantasy of escaping from this dangerous man.

Pregnant women have dreams about murderous men, but it is also quite common for them to have dreams about killing men and boy babies. Dreams like the one Annette had (see chapter 2, p. 33) about aborting a boy, highlight the fact that pregnancy tends to heighten aggression toward men. A common thought verbalized among pregnant women is, "I don't need a man in my life now. I've got the baby, and that's all I need." The discharge of this aggression into language can have a very beneficial effect on the progression of pregnancy, but not to a marriage or to a woman's relationship to all the important men in her life. An all-women's group of pregnant women can provide a safe environment to discharge the anger.

A Menopausal Group

A group composed of women in their late forties and early fifties amazed me by never talking about menopause. For the first two years of the life of the group, menopause seemed to be a taboo subject, and I wondered why it was never approached, since I was sure most of the women in the group were dealing with physical and emotional symptoms of the climacteric. Ruth was the first member to muster the courage to talk about this difficult subject.

She had been on a trip to Alaska with her adolescent daughter, during which they had fought bitterly. Ruth's daughter had constantly criticized Ruth on the vacation, and Ruth said, "I understand that she's adolescent, and usually I can be understanding, but lately I feel like I'm going mad. I have hot flashes and insomnia, and when you are sleep-deprived, it's hard to feel motherly or understanding." Ruth expressed guilt about talking about her difficulties to the group. I said, "What do you mean? You're supposed to say everything here." Through her tears, Ruth said,

> It's so wonderful to hear that. I can't talk about these things to men, because it's not sexy to be menopausal, and I'm afraid they'll think of me as an old hag and turn their attention to all the beautiful younger woman who seem to be everywhere these days. I can't talk about it with my children, because it will just bore them—or worse, scare them that their mother is going to get old and die. I feel like I remind everyone, including myself, of death. Even my best friend is no help. She won't even admit she's in menopause. She's just dealing with it with this rigid denial, and I feel so alone.

Ruth's honesty freed the rest of the group to begin speaking and suddenly, everyone was talking about the physical and emotional challenges they faced in this change of life. Alice, a very beautiful woman, talked about the narcissistic injury of watching your beauty fade, "I didn't realize what power there is in being beautiful until I began to lose that beauty." Edna, who had always considered herself "ugly," comforted Alice by saying, "I've never been beautiful, so I never knew that power. That's probably why I went to medical school and cultivated my intellect. And you can do that too, Alice. The fading of your beauty may force you to find other sources of power—like brains and wisdom." Several women expressed the idea that the grief and fear that menopause induces made them feel like a "burden" to everyone. But as they became freer to discuss their most painful thoughts, these feelings changed. Edna said to Ruth,

> You may feel like a burden to yourself, but you don't feel like a burden to me. In fact, listening to you makes me realize that maybe I'm not the burden I thought I was. Maybe I could risk talking to my husband about some of this. God knows I need his love and support right now. I've just been afraid I would be too much for him.

These middle-aged women were able to use their feminine tendency to identify to strengthen each other. They could say to each other, "Oh, I've felt just like that. I understand." Because of the female tendency to willingly take the object in, projective identifications between group members were very fluid and playful, and often, those projective identifications were articulated, transformed, and given back to the projector for recognition and reintegration into the self. "You don't have to defend and explain yourself to me," Alice said to Edna, "I'm not your critical mother, you know."

The women learned to separate and dis-identify with some of the more painful feelings in a way that was even more helpful than their empathy for each other. Betty said, "I feel like a witch, I cry like a maniac, and I look like a cow. All I want to do is withdraw." Edna said, "I've felt like that too. But it's so interesting to me to be able to totally identify with what you're saying and also realize that you *don't* look like a witch, a maniac, *or* a cow to me. So maybe that means I can feel all those things about myself and still remember that I may not *be* all the things I feel. Maybe they're just feelings." Because the women in this group could use each other in a variety of ways, both as an internal object and as an intersubjective other, their ego identities became strengthened and enriched.

Women in the pregnancy group described pregnancy as a "special club," and indeed there was a sense of exclusiveness and sanctity about the circle of women about to give birth, a conviction that no one but another pregnant woman could truly understand what they were experiencing. A member of the menopausal group laughingly called the group "a coven of witches huddled around the cauldron stirring our herbs and potions." Another member corrected her, "Not witches—wise women." An all-women's group at these challenging times in a woman's biological life can provide a safe space; indeed, these groups may be the only place that a woman can "say everything."

Women in Mixed-Gender Groups

Critics of single-sex groups argue that the world is heterosexual and that limiting group psychotherapy to one sex or the other is a resistance. The debate about single-sex versus mixed-gender groups is a lively one, with both sides energetically advocating for their position. The debate will no doubt rage on, and probably a choice about a group should always best be made on an individual rather than an ideological basis. Though I have argued that, for women with a certain type of character structure or a particular developmental challenge, a woman's group can be meaningful and life enhancing, women can also function very effectively in mixed-gender groups if group leaders are constantly vigilant regarding important differences in male and female functioning. Traditionally, more masculine attributes such as self-actualization and autonomous functioning have been the most important qualities of mental health, and the ego or "I" so highly valued in psychoanalysis can sometimes dominate in a mixed-gender group. But female development occurs in the context of mutuality, and the ego or self strives to be enhanced in connection to others (Miller 1976). The challenge in a group of both men and women is to help the men acknowledge and be comfortable with the essential need for human connection and relationship, while ensuring that the women's need for connection is expressed in mutually enhancing relationship, not subservient affiliation. While men may fear entrapment and engulfment in facing mutuality, women fear aggression and the loss of relationship that may be its consequence: Even success and achievement can make them feel dangerously isolated (Gilligan 1982). One of the advantages of a mixed-gender group, led by a leader sensitive to these sexual differences, is that both fears can be acknowledged, discussed, and worked through.

The issue for women, whether in single-sex or mixed-gender groups, is the management of the complex world of introjected objects that is responsible for the feminine tendency toward empathy and intuition. This talent for identification, which can often become compulsive, is woman's greatest strength and biggest problem. The challenge in any setting is to use her ability to connect with others in the service of her own ego and to develop the courage to verbalize her healthy aggression when identification and connection threaten to become oppressive. A useful technique in meeting this challenge is to encourage women to think about and express what they feel *toward* other group members, rather than what they feel *with* them. Often when encouraged in this way, women will discover that they have a negative feeling toward the person with whom they are in complete and compulsive identification. The expression of this negative feeling in words is the triumph of the self over the introjected object and can free a woman from the tyranny of her internal world. This triumph should be an important goal for both women's groups and women in groups.

CHAPTER SIX

Playing in a Women's Group

As any parent or teacher knows, play is one of the earliest ways that human beings mature and learn. When a child plays, she enters a world that integrates fantasy and reality, where she can manipulate objects according to her own imagination. She must be aware of the plaything, which represents reality, while exercising complete control over it in a pleasurable regression to primary narcissism and omnipotence. The toy or object is "not-me," but this "not-me" is subjugated by the "me"; thus, play expresses the wish that the separation between the "me" and the "not-me" does not exist (Winnicott 1953). The *play space* is an intermediate area between fantasy and reality, between the "me" and "not-me" where the object can be perceived as both outside of the child's omnipotent control and as an object of all the child's various projection. The bridge that play builds between fantasy and reality makes the sad fact of our own lack of control over the world more bearable.

D. W. Winnicott (1989) wrote extensively on the value of play. He described it as a creative way to deal with external reality, which ultimately produces creative living and leads to the capacity to feel real and to feel life can be used and enriched (undated, 59–60). Play is always exciting because it deals with the precarious borderline between the subjective and what can be objectively perceived, creating an experience of separation without separation (Winnicott 1964, 146). In play, the child not only takes in the world for integration, but, through manipulating objects in an area somewhere between fantasy and reality, also reveals who she is.

Winnicott (1989, 59) described the satisfaction of play as dependent on the use of symbols. When a child plays, *this* stands for *that*. If *that* is loved, *this* can be used and enjoyed. If *that* is hated, then *this* can be knocked over, killed and restored, and killed again. Play is an expression of identification with other persons. To really play, a child must have developed a capacity to use objects. Play becomes a crucial part of the transition from the primary process of infancy to the reality principle.

Play therapy, in which play does the work of free association in adult psychoanalysis, has been the treatment of choice for children since the early days of psychoanalysis. Melanie Klein discovered that the child expresses her fantasies and real-life experiences in symbolic expression through play. Play can be analyzed as a symptom or dream can be analyzed. The child also talks as she plays, and these words are like free association. For Klein, play reveals the unconscious in childhood analysis in the same way that "saying everything" does in the analysis of adults (Kaplan and Sadock 1981, 163).

Winnicott (1971) asserted that the concept of play therapy is useful in adult analysis as well. He recommended that the analyst play with the patient by putting forth, not an interpretation in the classical sense, but an idea about the patient that can exist as an object of play between the analyst and the patient. Chodorow (1999) described the analyst and the patient as together creating an analytic third in the potential space between them. In this *play space*, meaning is created through interactions that include playing with projective and introjective identification, object usage, transitional meanings, and objects created by one or the other person. Many aspects—the fluid process of lively interchange between the inner and the outer world, the continual projective identifications that allocate parts of the self to the other, and the introjective identifications which draw parts of the other into the self—become a sort of enriching play that facilitates the maturation of both analyst and patient, liberating the power of both party's feelings.

Female patients are particularly good at this kind of play. Because women use introjection of objects as a way to feel power and control, they are usually highly skilled at playing with their own internalized objects and accepting the projections and fantasies of others. In particular, women's groups can be a powerful vehicle for the creation of a nurturing play space for their members.

Anna Freud (1960) described the maturational sequence of play in young children. Originally, play is parallel; very young children may play side by side, but the play is individual and utilizes a toy or object that is individually pleasing. When young children become aware of other children, they usually treat them as a toy that can be used, mistreated, and then pushed away. It is through play, in which others are fitted into preconceived roles, that the child begins to allow others to have independent existences (Winnicott 1964, 144). By the end of the second year of life, most children are capable of seeing others as playmates who can be helpful in achieving a common wish of either building or destroying something together. Thus in play, we trace human development from inner reality to shared reality, from egocentricity to companionship (Freud 1965).

This progression of play from narcissism to object relatedness is often reflected in group dynamics. Early in the life of a group, the analyst observes an assemblage of people who simply want to play alone. Every member has a "story" to relate, usually focusing on the way the world and the people in it have been a source of disappointment or pain. Each wants to play with her story/toy by talking about it with very little awareness that there are other potential playmates in the room. If there is any object awareness at all, it is usually of the analyst, but commonly she is perceived not as a real and separate object, but as a toy to be used. Of course, to play well, a patient needs to develop a capacity to recognize and use objects. Play in the group becomes a crucial part of the transition from the primary process of narcissism to the reality principle.

The analyst encourages this transition by being patient with the process, allowing the patient to be alone with her story/toy initially, while always encouraging her to use the analyst and other members as external ports for all her fantasies and projections. Eventually, the patient may be willing to give up her narcissism and become more object-oriented. When the patient feels ready to play with the analyst and other members, the story/toy may become less important than the here and now of the group. She is ready to tell the group her immediate thoughts and feelings about the other group members and the analyst. The group can begin to play with the patient by putting forth ideas as objects that exist, not in the patient nor in the analyst, but in that potential play space between the two. The patient plays with the group by projecting early objects onto and into other members. The analyst identifies and attempts to understand these projections but inevitably through the filter of her own subjective experience. What the analyst gives back to the patient are the patient's projections altered and played with by the analyst's ideas. The playful toss back and forth of introjection and projection liberates feelings and helps the group members and the analyst say new things. In this playful atmosphere, the group bounces around themes, metaphors, and dreams.

As the group progresses and all the members become more interested in the other people in the room than in their own story/toy, the analytic play space starts to take shape and belong to everyone. An intermediate area between fantasy and reality, this play space allows group members to perceive each other as both outside each other's omnipotent control and yet willing to receive and play with the various projections and fantasies of the other. Each member can bring along the spirits of all her internal objects and transfer them to a receptive place in other members. Though it is difficult to describe, a profound experience can occur in the group play space as one person moves through another, "like a ghost moving through the internal objects in the room of the other's mind" (Bollas 1992, 56). When groups are able to play in this way, the leader helps members have fun with themes that arise in the room. She encourages the kind of progressive emotional communication between members in the here and now that is always more valued than a focus on the past or explanation or insight from the analyst (Ormont 1997, 59). Because encouraging group members to live and play in the moment keeps a group alive, the leader constantly encourages the group to speak in the present tense, rather than going back to the narcissistic play of focusing on the past (Ormont 2001, 104–5). When the group plays by focusing on their thoughts and feeling toward each other rather than their own story/toy, opportunities arise for each group member to reveal old defenses and resistances not by reporting them, but by experiencing them in the present. Playful immediacy can also facilitate the revelation of new features of each member's character and the chance to move relationships to new levels (Ormont 2001, 378). Like children constructing block houses, members begin to build bridges of ever-deepening meaning in a game of interaction and relationship that enriches all the players. In this playful interchange, the group becomes a collective genius, more brilliant than the analyst or any of its members.

In one of my groups, the members played with, and gave meaning to, the theme of water. After Jane compared her relationship with her boyfriend with scuba diving ("I totally immerse myself in him. It's exhilarating as long as you can come up for air."), other group members began to use water metaphors as a method of communication. They felt "engulfed" and "drowned" by their children, their mates, their careers. They encouraged each other to "just go with the flow." A quiet group member said she was standing on the beach holding her towel, watching the others swim. The other members encouraged her to just "jump in." She couldn't—the water was too hot and turbulent and she was afraid she would never get out again. Someone suggested that I, as group leader, should play lifeguard. On evenings when the group was muted and overly intellectual, someone would remark that the water was "too cold tonight." Playing in the water was a step toward helping group members become more articulate about their feelings.

Playing with Dreams

Dreams can be wonderful toys in analysis. Bollas (1987) talked about the dream as a place for the interplay of self and other. The dreams of group members and the analyst's response to them can provide a fertile ground for the development of playful, metaphorical communication within the group. A dream offers an opportunity to deepen the group process and make it come alive.

When a group member presents a dream, it can be tempting for the leader to focus on that member on a one-to-one basis to methodically analyze the dream. Classical analysts would probably offer interpretations to analyze the dream presented by a group member. But proceeding in this way prohibits the kind of progressive, emotional communication between members that can occur when the leader brings the whole group into the discussion. A modern group analyst will do better to treat the dream as a toy to be shared by all the members. No longer the exclusive possession of the dreamer, the dream can receive a multitude of fantasies, projections, and identifications. When the leader is careful to include all the members, the dream becomes a group property (Livingston 2001, 16–25).

I had a patient, Mary, in group who was terrified of aggression, especially her own. After several years of sitting with this gentle airy-fairy and joining her resistance by being very, very nice, I began to get impatient with her defenses and started to make some provocative interventions to see if I could move her along in getting in touch with her anger. In response to this change in my treatment plan, she came in with a dream. She was with a black woman who was speaking softly and supposedly lovingly, touching her in a pseudo-gentle way. But in her hand, this woman had a needle, and she stuck Mary in the leg with it and screamed, "You must have an orgasm." Mary screamed, "I can't! I can't."

Mary's association to the dream was that I was the pseudo-gentle black woman who was demanding orgasms. I agreed that I should stop needling her, but another member of the group thought that this pseudo-gentle black woman might also represent Mary herself, and the group played with the idea that there might be a part of Mary that was as angry and impatient as the woman in the dream. The group did a good job of exploring this with Mary. Because they used humor to "play" with the idea, and also because they identified with Mary's need to be "nice," they were gentle with her. Someone said, "Gee, Mary, maybe if you got angry, I might be able to have an orgasm. My husband will be eternally grateful to you!" Mary was able to play with the idea of herself as angry and needling without feeling defensive, and this had the effect of allowing Mary to be comfortable and playful not only with her own aggression, but with the aggression of the other members.

That night, I dreamed that Mary and I were taking a test, and we were both having difficulty with it. Mary created the test, but neither one of us could answer the questions. There was a woman in the dream who had already finished the test and she was very harsh. She told us that we only had a half-hour to finish the test, and if we couldn't, we both would fail. While Mary and I struggled to answer the questions, the other woman was talking and talking much too loudly, and it was impossible to concentrate. I said to the woman, "Please be quiet! We will never pass, if you don't stop talking!"

I played with these two dreams for many weeks in my own head. I was amused by the fact that Mary's angry black woman had decided to visit my dream, and this time was needling us both. I enjoyed the idea that, in my dream, I had told this woman (who was probably me) to be quiet. While Mary talked in the group, I silently thought about the test that we both might fail, and about how much she induced in me the desire to be noisy. I also thought about the part of Mary that creates such a difficult test that we both struggle with.

In the group, the members played with the idea that I "needle" people. After Mary reported her dream, they had no problem expressing their annoyance with me if I seemed to be prodding someone to have a metaphorical orgasm. "Don't rush her! She doesn't need an injection, Doctor!," someone would say to me if I was making demands on a member to be more immediate and emotionally present. But they also played with Mary, confronting her with her "pseudo-gentleness." The group continued to encourage Mary to get more comfortable with the aggressive woman in her dream, and to confront me when I was trying to poke her. Eventually, Mary was able to play with me, always in a lighthearted way, about which of us was the most aggressive under our "feminine" exteriors.

Freud (1905, 228) characterized humor as man's "highest psychical achievement." Jokes and humor give us a life-affirming way of discharging primitive sex and aggression while preventing the actual acting out of these feelings. We can discharge toxic impulses in a way that gives us relief without anyone actually getting harmed. The use of humor is vital in helping patients deal with the primitive impulses that are aroused in group and which often frighten and overstimulate the members.

Playing with Murder

In a supervision group, the members were able to toss some murderous aggression around by using play and humor. An analyst, I'll call her Doris, was talking about a male patient she was having difficulty with. "The problem is I'd like to kill him. He reminds me of my ex-husband. Truthfully, if I thought I could kill them both and get away with it, I would." Doris blushed and said, "I can't believe I could even entertain the idea of actually murdering someone."

Anne, another analyst in the group said, "Doris, you need to go see my Babushka. She's my Russian grandmother, and she casts spells on people." Anne went on to explain:

> Baba went to a family wedding, and she didn't like the way my cousin was dancing with this young woman in a very short skirt. She said it was unseemly. So she went home and put a curse on the young man. Sure enough, my cousin began to get sick. He lost weight and couldn't eat. He went to the doctor, but they couldn't find anything wrong with him. His mother called my Babushka and said she didn't know what to do, she was at her wit's end. Baba said, "The only thing wrong with him is that I put a curse on him and now he sees what happens to young men who behave in brazen ways to disgrace our family!" My aunt said, "Baba, stop it! Take the curse off." My grandmother said, "I won't! He's only getting what he deserves!" Well, my cousin got sicker and sicker, and his mother called my grandmother back, and said, "Baba—are you trying to kill him? He's very sick." My grandmother said, "Oh, all right. I guess I don't want to see him dead. I'll take the curse off." And she did, and my cousin recovered. "You need my Babushka, Doris."

Doris' eyes got very wide with pleasure and anxiety, and she said, "You mean your Babushka could put a curse on my ex-husband, and he would *die?*"

Anne nodded gravely, "I'm pretty sure she could do it."

Doris said, "This is terrible. I can't believe I'm entertaining this idea. Would she see me?"

Anne said, "I'm sure she would do it if she knew you were a good friend of mine."

Doris giggled nervously, "I could really arrange my ex-husband's death and actually get away with it? Oh God, I can't believe I'm talking like this. I couldn't do that. I would feel so guilty. No, it would never work. I would probably have to give myself cancer in punishment for being a murderer."

"Don't be ridiculous," said Anne, "you would have no reason to feel guilty at all. All this black magic is a bunch of hocus-pocus bullshit anyway!"

At this, Doris started to laugh. She laughed and then she began to cry. She said, "Playing with murder is so therapeutic! I wish I knew why I'm crying." Her laughter and tears seemed to me to be a release of all the toxic primitive feelings that were overwhelming her—the wish to murder, the self-destructive guilt, the shame at her own aggression, the horrible feelings toward her patient. All of this, she was able to play with and let go.

In the group the following week, Doris talked about her play with Anne,

> The laughter helped me understand something important. All this horrible stuff within me—it's all just feelings. I can laugh about it, share it with friends in a playful way, and then decide how I want to operate in the world vis-à-vis my patient and the father of my children. I can know the basest thing about myself and forgive myself. And the interesting thing is, forgiving myself makes it easier for me to understand and forgive my patient and my ex-husband.

Humor and play help human beings face and cope with their own primitive aggression, so that it doesn't have to be acted out in the world in destructive ways. Doris went on to say, "I can enjoy my murderous fantasies. Now I know I can use them—sort of like the cayenne pepper in a stew—to enliven my life, you know, increase its savor."

CHAPTER SEVEN

Hell Hath No Fury: How Women Seek Revenge

Getting even, if done correctly, is one of life's greatest pleasures. An important goal for any analysis is to help the patient get even in ways that give her pleasure and don't land her in jail or in the back ward of a mental hospital. Although all human beings savor revenge, most unfortunately seek it with unconscious and primitive methods that cause them at least as much suffering as the objects they are out to get. Beginning an analysis can often be the first step toward constructive retribution but, as we know, it is an arduous, often painful process, which requires courage and fortitude. The best revenge takes time and patience, but in psychoanalysis, we begin the first time we come to the analyst's office to report the crime.

When I think about the women I have listened to in the treatment room, three modes of seeking revenge emerge as favored by females: women suffer, they seduce, and they repeat through identification. I have known several gifted women who have been able to do all three at once. Although there is enormous secondary gain in all three of these methods, they each have major drawbacks to the patient, which I will discuss.

Suffering is probably the least satisfying and most self-destructive way a woman can get even, but it is very popular; I think it is safe to say that it is more common among women than men, except perhaps in the case of schizophrenia. The degree of female suffering is widely variable. One of my female patients is married to a very wealthy and very controlling man, who dotes on her by buying her beautiful clothes and jewelry, taking her on trips, and constantly redecorating their house in the Caribbean and their

New York apartment. All of this makes his wife miserable. She is tired, bored, and listless. The husband, a retired businessman, has boundless energy. He wants to go to parties every night. He wants to go to China and India and South America. My patient feels tortured by this. Her favorite pastime is lying in bed reading women's magazines. She needs a lot of sleep. Her husband brings home Valentino suits. She weeps in response, worrying about money. He forces her to make dinner dates with other couples every night of the week, but she thwarts him both by arguing with or insulting the women and coquettishly confessing to the men that her husband won't have sex with her. Not surprisingly, their social dance card is getting shorter and shorter, which tortures the husband. In fact, these two have spent almost forty years of their married life torturing each other.

Lately, however, I have noticed that my patient's suffering seems to be winning the battle over her husband's control, because the husband is getting sicker and sicker, and now the wife is afraid he is going to die. Is this a wish, the final triumph of her revenge? Or is she genuinely afraid that he will die, and she will lose the object she has been enjoying getting even with all these years? I suspect that if she does manage to kill him with her suffering, she is going to get very depressed, despite her triumph. Relatedly, this woman gets even with me by never making any progress. This tortures me. I find I have plans for her, just like her husband, and her refusal to go along with my plans tortures me. In the eighth year of treatment she told me, "The problem is my husband and my marriage, and I am not going to get rid of him, so there's nothing you can do about any of this. You're stuck, and I'm stuck." I said, "Okay then—I guess all we're going to do is talk."

Of course, it is tempting for the analyst to think, "We should all suffer like this woman," and when I do think that, I tell myself that I have a point. But on the other hand, I know she would get much more pleasure out of life if she gave up her aggressive suffering and followed my plans for her. I want her to torture her husband by going back to school and finding some friends where the relationship is not based on who has the largest diamond ring. I would like her to be an analyst like me. She's not going to do any of this because it is too much fun to torture me for wanting to control her, just like that irritating husband of hers.

Revengeful suffering can be pretty gruesome. Some women are willing to destroy their lives just to show the world what horrible mothers and analysts they have had to endure. I have worked for twenty years with a woman who arrives for each session twenty minutes late. She comes in and spends the next twenty minutes berating herself for never being able to get anywhere on time. In the first few years of treatment, she lost job after job because of her lateness, going from being a copyeditor at a newspaper to being a house cleaner. She lost her apartment and had to move into a single-room occupancy hotel. All the while, she was spending her thirty-minute session beating her breast about how defective she is. I told her the problem was not her. The problem was that she had a defective analyst. When she tortured me by telling me what a failure she is, I told her we were a perfect match, because I was a total failure as an analyst.

In the fifth year of treatment, this patient started talking about suicide. At this point, I was feeling rather suicidal myself. I was fairly new at analyzing patients then, and I was ready to give it all up and jump out the window, so I went to supervision. My supervisor told me to tell this woman that she shouldn't kill herself. She should kill me, because I was the problem. I followed my supervisor's advice and I noticed that it worked rather well. My patient reassured me that she could never contemplate murdering me, but she seemed pleased with the idea, and she began to get better. She got a job as a companion to a rich old man who fell in love with her and wanted to marry her. He moved her out of the dreary old SRO into a nice sunny studio and took her to Europe. She refused his offer of marriage but she managed to keep this job for three years and get herself out of debt.

So I decided to raise her fee by five dollars. When I told her, she said, "Well, I guess it's okay. Things have been going better for me, and you've never raised my fee before." But the next thing she told me after the raise in fee was that she was arguing with the old man. He was getting unbearably crabby because she was arriving two hours late to take him to the movies. After a few weeks of this, he threw her out, fired her as his companion, and stopped paying her rent. Back she went to the SRO and, as a result, she stopped paying me. We talked at length about what was going on in her life and when she planned to bring me some money; but when her bill reached $1,000, I told her we were going to have to take a break until she could pay what she owed me.

Though the song was ended, the melody lingered on, at least in my mind. I tortured myself for months about how I failed this woman. I thought about giving up the idea of being a psychoanalyst. I contemplated downsizing apartments myself, since I couldn't even get people to pay me. My only consolation was that I fully believed that I would never see the patient, let alone her money, again, and the idea of not being tortured every week gave me pleasure.

Two years went by, and to my surprise, I got a check for $1,000 from my patient followed by a phone call. She wanted to come back into analysis. With misgivings, I agreed. The patient came to my office and told me that since she left analysis, her life has been wonderful. All the credit for this transformation, she gave to me. While she had been away, I had been constantly in her mind. Psychoanalysis was responsible for the fact that she now had a good job as a proofreader and was able to afford to pay her own rent on another sunny studio. She wanted to resume the analysis because now she wanted a relationship with a man.

Since then, this patient has been getting even with me by engaging in anonymous and masochistic one-night stands. I have been tortured by this. I feel that not only am I a terrible analyst but I also may be responsible for her possible future death from some STD. The only time she has managed to have a fairly constructive relationship with a man was the time we had to take another break in the treatment because of an unpaid bill. It seems this woman can only prosper when she is away from me. I have pointed this out to her and asked if perhaps I am the wrong analyst for her. She insists that I am the perfect analyst for her.

Lately, I have been asking my patient how she would like me to feel about her sexual activities. The thought that I might have feelings about her life is entirely novel to her. It will be interesting to see if she will have to leave me again to have a more productive sexual relationship. I suspect she will, since it would give me too much pleasure to know she has stopped being promiscuous.

So I think we've suffered enough with suffering. Let's talk about seduction, which is another favorite female method of getting revenge. Seduction is much more fun than suffering and it is highly effective as a form of revenge. The personal cost of seduction is not as high as suffering, though there is still a cost. Women have been using seduction to destroy the object since long before the sirens lured sailors to their death—but seduction as a dynamic in analysis has certain characteristics. The patient is usually, though not always, physically attractive. There is always an idealized transference to the analyst. The patient needs protection; she presents as extraordinarily vulnerable and delicate. She needs saving and the analyst gets the idea that she can and should be a savior. My problem with patients like this has been that I love them too much, and when I love them too much, they always kill me off. In supervision when I talk about a countertransference of excessive worry or concern—or about nameless longings—my supervisor always has to remind me that the sweet young thing on my couch is a potential murderer.

Let me tell you about Eve. Eve is a ballet dancer. When she came for a consultation, the first thing she said to me was "Seven people are in love with me." I could see why. She was beautiful, delicate, angelic looking. She was also full of feeling and very articulate. She cried easily. I wanted to take care of Eve and she gave me the idea that I was perfect for the job. She called me a "wise woman" and a "goddess." She wrote a lovely poem about me and brought it to her session. She said that analysis was going to save her life.

Eve had a very sad history. Her father was an alcoholic and her mother was a heroin addict. She had been raped by a friend of her father's when she was fifteen years old. I longed to be her "good enough" mother.

Eve dreamed and reported her dreams frequently. I always found them rather beautiful. She dreamed her father had taken her room from her. He took all her books and pictures from the shelves and filled them with bottles of alcohol. She looked for her diary and realized that her mother had stolen it. Her mother was there and said, "I didn't steal it. It's mine. Your thoughts and dreams belong to me."

In another dream, Eve and her female roommate, to whom she said she felt sexually attracted, were swept away in a tidal wave. The wave threw Eve down and broke every bone in her body. A fireman, who was big and strong but like a robot, tied a rope around her ankles and rescued her by pulling her out. She wanted to have sex with him, but when she tried to embrace him, she couldn't move. Another man was there watching.

One day in the second year of her analysis, Eve came in and told me that she had gotten a job touring with a ballet company for the summer. She was going to take a three-month break from treatment. I suggested that we have phone sessions while she was away but she refused. Really, she couldn't even consider the idea. Her mind was already on the road and she had shed me and the analysis as easily as a butterfly sheds the cocoon. And so she left. While she was away, I missed her terribly. I worried about her excessively. I received one letter, telling me how much she missed me and recounting what she was experiencing, all with the charm of Scheherazade and her Arabian tales.

One day after her return to analysis, Eve came in to tell me that she had had a very unsettling dream. She had dreamed that she and I had sex. She said, "I'm not a homosexual. How could I dream such a thing?" I said, "What's wrong with that dream?" Eve began to weep. She said, "I guess I'm so ashamed because the truth is I do love you and would like to have sex with you." What I said next was one of the big mistakes of my analytic career: good intervention but about thirty years too soon. I said, "That's a nice fantasy."

There was a long silence. Then Eve sat up on the couch with a look on her face that truly frightened me. In that moment, I was completely scared of her. She looked psychotic, sexual, and murderous. She looked at me through lowered lids and said, "What are you trying to do to me?" I said, "What is it?"

She said, "What are you trying to do to me? Do you want to sleep with me?" I said, "All we're going to do here is talk." She said, "What do you think I am, some kind of pervert?" Then I think I said something intelligent like, "What do you mean?" Eve stood up and said, "I have to get out of here." I said, "The session is not over." She said, "I have to get out of here. You're trying to turn me into a lesbian." I said, "I think we need to talk about this. All we're going to do is talk, right?" She said, "I know what you're up to." I said, "What is it?" She said, "What they're all up to, that's what. I have to go." And she left.

I never saw Eve again. She never answered my calls. I was never able to get her on the phone. I wrote a letter telling her I thought the treatment had reached a crucial place and invited her in to talk. She never responded. For months, I tortured myself. I was a terrible analyst. Eve should sue me for malpractice. I was responsible for making her psychotic. My heart was broken.

Eve has gone on to become rather famous. I read about her in the arts section of the *New York Times* frequently. I'm sure she is still breaking hearts.

The problem with seduction as a way to get even is that it makes for a rather arid life. These sexy women are rarely sexual. All libido goes into being lovable to the object and there is really no energy left to love. Ormont (personal conversation) once reminded me that babies need to be loved but, for adults, a happy and meaningful life comes not from being loved, but from loving. The older I get, the more I realize this is true, though I might add that it helps to love people who aren't too invested in killing you off. Seductive people are really imprisoned by their own narcissism—and by the way, they get old very ungracefully, which I guess is our revenge on them.

Now I want to move to what I consider the most fascinating and creative way that women get even—by identifying with the object. The internal triangle is deeply implicated in this tendency. Women use their parental imagoes in all sorts of interesting ways, but one of the most useful ones is to express aggression more or less unconsciously. Let me tell you about a woman who used her unconscious identification with her parental introjects, not only to get even with me but also to try to destroy my group.

Heidi came to my office because she had heard that I had women's groups. She had just left another group led by a man with whom she was very angry. She had decided that she needed to be in an all-female environment. Heidi had a rather lurid history. Her father, a prominent psychiatrist in Denmark, had had sex with each of Heidi's four sisters. Heidi was the only child who had been spared this treatment, and Heidi reported that this was because she was the youngest of the five daughters, and her mother had sent her father the unconscious message: "Don't you touch this one. She belongs to me."

Heidi idealized her mother. She described her as a "saint who bore everything with dignity." This, despite the fact that the mother had never believed Heidi when she tried to tell her about the incest that was going on right under her nose. Heidi grew up in a house of secrets. Her sisters tearfully begged Heidi not to tell or talk. They were afraid the father would kill them all. When teenager Heidi tried to confront her father, he vehemently denied any wrongdoing and told her she was crazy. Heidi said, "I was the only one who knew everything. I held all the secrets."

At first, Heidi seemed to love the group. She talked about how liberating it was to know, for the first time, that she could really feel and say everything. Heidi had a very volatile temperament. She could easily fly into a rage if any other member of the group provoked her. Though she could be frightening, I felt Heidi needed protection when she was this angry, and I always tried to direct her anger at me. When I added a new member to the group, Heidi assaulted her. I said, "Listen, Heidi, you shouldn't be mad at Jennifer. You should be mad at me. I'm the one who added a new member." Heidi turned to me and said, "You! I'd like to cut out your uterus." Other members of the group expressed horror at this idea, but I said, "What do you mean? That's a very creative image. How should a child feel when a mother has a new baby?" This seemed to make Heidi feel very safe for a while. She told me how wonderful it was to finally have a therapist who wasn't afraid of her anger. She relished telling me she would like to "cut my tongue out" when I said something that annoyed her. She realized for the first time that she had other feelings toward her mother, whom she had idealized and protected in her dangerous family.

So at first, Heidi had no problem with me. Her problem was with the other women. Heidi managed to isolate herself in the group by frightening most of the other members with her rages. Until Heidi had arrived, this had been a group that had a fairly entrenched resistance, which expressed itself in a compulsion to be "helpful" and in a denial that any aggression existed at all. Heidi, of course, flew in the face of this resistance and, suddenly, I had a management problem on my hands. When Heidi expressed rage toward me, the other members rushed to protect me, and they worked hard to make Heidi feel guilty. They told her she was "too angry," that she was using anger to defend against other feelings. Though probably true, these interpretations induced even more rage in Heidi. She began to feel that, like her mother, I couldn't protect her. She saw herself as the "container for the truth" in the group. The other members and I were in a conspiracy against her.

Then I made another mistake, which cost me dearly. I put a new member into this group without adequate preparation. A psychiatrist friend of mine, a woman I trusted, sent me a referral. The psychiatrist said Angela would be wonderful for my group. She was articulate, a poet, mother to a new baby girl. The psychiatrist had worked with her for several years. Angela had decided she wanted a group and so she was sent to me. I interviewed Angela once, and she did seem perfect for my group. The group needed new members, so I put her right in.

Angela arrived for her first group session. She told everyone about her poetry and her new baby girl, and then she said, "I'm planning to end my life this week." There was a long, astonished silence, which I broke by asking, "Do you have a plan for ending your life?" Angela said yes, indeed, she did. She said, "I have a bottle of sleeping pills and a quart of vodka, and Friday night when my husband and daughter go to temple, I'm going to kill myself."

Well, as you can imagine, most of the rest of the group was spent on trying to save Angela from herself. I felt like a suicide bomber had come into my office and was threatening to blow us all up. I felt scared and very angry. I asked Angela if we could have a contract that she would hold off on her suicide and agree to come back to group next week. She said she couldn't be sure she could promise that.

And sure enough, on Saturday morning, I got a call from Angela. She said, "I won't be able to make group on Tuesday night. I'm in intensive care. I tried to kill myself on Friday night, but I didn't succeed. I'll be back to group a week from Tuesday. Please tell the group what happened, and tell everyone I said hi!"

The next group was very lively indeed. When I announced that Angela had made an unsuccessful suicide attempt and would see us all next week, most of the group was furious. Happily, this event seemed to resolve the group resistance to aggression. All these lovely, polite women were finally angry with me. One said, "How dare you do this to us? How could you put someone in here who is suicidal? I feel like you tried to murder us all by putting Angela in this group."

Interestingly enough though, Heidi, the usual container for the aggression, had another reaction. She burst into tears and said, "Oh poor Angela! I loved her. She was wonderful. She's a person who's comfortable with primitive feelings. I felt we were soul mates. What hospital is she in? I want to call her and tell her to come back as soon as she can."

Janet, another member of the group, said, "What! No way is she coming back! I don't want her here. She's a killer." Beth said, "If she wants to kill herself, I wish she could at least be good at it." Beth was immediately chastised for this remark by some of the more upstanding members of the group, but Emily supported Beth. She said, "I'm furious at Angela, and there's a part of me that wishes she had succeeded."

Heidi said, "How can you say that? Angela needs help, and we can help her. My sister tried to kill herself when my father raped her. Have a heart. Have some compassion!"

The rest of the group was devoted to the question: Should I allow Angela to come back to group? I was reluctant to agree to this. At one point, Heidi turned to me and said, "You seem so angry at Angela, Lucy." I said, "How should I feel about suicide? Should I be pleased?"

In the end, Heidi was so assertive in her insistence that the group could help Angela and that we couldn't abandon her, that it was agreed that Angela could come back. And she did. The next week she told the group that her suicide attempt had been an epiphany, a turning point in her life. She had acted out her mother's wish to destroy her and now she realized she wanted to live. She wanted to make a commitment to the group.

Heidi was jubilant. She said, "I am so glad. I feel so close to you. I feel at last I have a companion who understands my primitive feelings. I know we can help each other, and you shouldn't worry about what Beth and Emily said about you." Angela said, "What did they say about me?" Heidi said, "Oh, nothing. It isn't important. What's important is that you're here."

But Angela was not to be deterred. She turned to Beth and Emily and said, "What did you say about me?"

Emily and Beth were both very flustered. They told Angela they couldn't remember what they had said, only that they had been very, very upset at her suicide attempt. Angela turned again to Heidi, "Tell me what they said." Heidi said, "They may not remember, but I know the truth. I know what they said about you, but I can't tell. It's too painful. I'm afraid you'll use it to attack yourself."

So now we had an interesting dynamic. Heidi knew the "truth" about the other women but it was too painful to reveal. This situation played itself out over several weeks. Angela wanted to know Heidi's secret. She put pressure on all of us to reveal the secret. Emily and Beth continued to assert that they couldn't even remember what they said, and that it wasn't important. I tried to explore with Angela why it was so important that we reconstruct the session she had missed. Angela said she couldn't stay in a group where people said bad things about her. I asked her if it would be all right if people didn't have good feelings about her suicide attempt. She said maybe so but the feeling she wanted to induce in the group was concern. Heidi said, "Concern, ha!"

And so we arrived at the climax of this little drama. Angela came into group one night and confronted Heidi. She said, "I want you to tell me what was said about me in the week that I was away." I intervened and said, "Are we going to take Heidi's version of what was said or Emily and Beth's version of what was said as the truth?"

Heidi turned on me in a rage, "I know the truth. You may want to protect Emily and Beth and yourself, but I know the truth. Don't try to tell me I don't. Emily and Beth said they wished Angela had succeeded in killing herself, and Lucy agreed!" Emily said, "Oh, I don't think I said that. That doesn't sound like me. That's just not my style." Heidi turned on Emily, "How dare you! My memory is excellent! I never forget anything that was said." I asked, "And what if others have a different memory?" Heidi said, "They may choose to forget, but I know I remember accurately. I can't help it if others can't face the truth." I turned to Angela and said, "Heidi's reality is the one true reality here." Heidi said, "I don't appreciate your sarcasm, Lucy. And that isn't all, Angela. Lucy said you are a big fat pig who monopolized the conversation." At this point, I'm afraid I lost my analytic neutrality. "I absolutely refute that!" I yelled. Heidi stood up and said, "How dare you call me a liar." I invited her to sit down. Emily said, "There's something toxic in this room, and it's dangerous because it's indirect. You may be the container for the truth, Heidi, but I feel you want to sit back while we all murder each other."

Though I was shaking, I stood to end the session and said, "This was a lively group. There were lots of angry feelings, and everyone did a great job of putting them into words."

Suicidal Angela went on to have many more productive sessions in the group. She became much less depressed and finally left the group after the birth of her second child. Heidi, however, did not fare so well. She came back to group for a few more sessions, but said, "I am exhausted by my own anger. I have turned this group into my original family, and I cannot stay." Though I told her that the problem was mine; that I, like her mother, had not wanted to hear the truth and had not protected her from the other members of the family, Heidi seemed worn out and defeated. She left the group.

But the story is not over. A few months later, one of the members of this group came in and made a guilty confession. "I had dinner with Heidi last night. I know it's against the rules, but she's been calling me since she left, wanting to be my friend and go to the movies. Finally, I agreed to go out to dinner, and we had a wonderful time!"

Beth said, "That's funny. Heidi's been calling me too. I told her the group contract is no outside contact, but she said she's no longer a member of the group, so the rule doesn't apply to her. So far, I've resisted."

Another member said, "Well, I didn't. I did go to the movies with Heidi. I felt so guilty about it that I didn't dare bring it up, but since it's on the table . . ." Emily said, "I can't believe this. Heidi's been calling me too. She said Lucy's rule is ridiculous, and anyway, a friendship is more meaningful than the group is."

A discussion followed about whether or not my rule was ridiculous. I said, "Should I modify the rule? Perhaps I should say it's okay to have dinner but no sex. Or maybe sex is okay too. What do you think, Emily? Should we all have sex with Heidi? Or should everyone but me have sex with Heidi? I guess I won't be able to have sex with her, since I'm the only one she hasn't contacted." Angela said, "That's not true. She hasn't contacted me." Emily said, "Maybe that's because you're her soul mate." I said, "What do you say, Beth? Should Heidi have sex with everyone but me and Angela? What do you think she's trying to communicate to us?"

The group was able to work through this issue, and it was finally agreed that the members would adhere to my rule and suggest to Heidi that if she wanted contact, she should come back to the group. Heidi never called to ask to return, but I did hear from her recently, right after this twelve-year-long group ended. A few weeks after the group agreed to disband, I got a call from Heidi. She said, "I heard your group ended. You must be very sad." I said, "On the contrary. I feel very satisfied that the group was able to survive for twelve years, and that I learned so much from all of you." Heidi said, "Well, I just wanted you to know that I think it's too bad that it fell apart."

In the years I have practiced analysis, I have seen many women act out their rage in unconscious identification with one parent or the other, but I think it is safe to say that Heidi was the most dramatic example. Not only did she arrange to repeat her original family dynamic in the group—with me cast as the consciously adored and unconsciously reviled mother—but she was also able to morph into her incestuous father and show me how it felt to be the only one who wasn't chosen.

In spite of these cases, which present some of my less stellar moments as a therapist, I have had some successes in helping women seek revenge in more constructive ways. I think of the schizophrenic who is now a rather brilliant schoolteacher. Sorry to say, her mother is dead, but I'm sure she would have been disappointed. Then I worked with a woman who was jilted by her husband and suicidal when she came into treatment. She is now happily remarried to a much richer and much younger husband and has had the pleasure of watching her ex-husband go through three more marriages. A woman who spent most of her life acting like a Barbie doll in unconscious compliance with her father, who thought of her as "a sexy little birdbrain," has recently finished her doctorate. The difference with these cases was the evolution of the transference. These success stories were able to give up the pleasure of destroying the object. Self-enhancement as a form of revenge then became an enticing alternative. Cure, after all, is the ultimate revenge.

CHAPTER EIGHT

The Mind of the Mother

I have a patient, a very nice woman, who suffers from anxiety attacks. Usually charming, articulate, and good natured, she becomes a different person when the attacks occur. At these times, she leaves repetitive messages on my voice mail in the middle of the night that are nothing more than wordless sobs. When she is able to speak, she calls back and threatens suicide. She becomes enraged that I don't immediately respond to these nocturnal cries of anguish. To complicate matters, the attacks usually occur when I am on vacation. In the treatment, I have been working with her to agree to wait to fall apart until I get home. Recently, she has been able to cooperate with this plan and bring her anxiety attacks into the session. She weeps and tells me she is going to lose her home and end up poor and alone on the street in the snow. She says that her planned knee surgery is going to fail and she will be confined to a wheelchair for the rest of her life. Her divorce, which has dragged on for four years, is never going to be final—she will be manipulated by her ex-husband until the day she dies, and there is nothing she or I can do about it. Though she presents herself as a helpless victim, her eyes are narrow and angry when she is in this state, and I respond by feeling tortured. Sometimes she stops sobbing, sits up, and snarls at me, "Do I have a sign on me that says *Abuse me*!?" When this happens, I feel that I am her abuser, that she is trying to kill me with her suffering, and I want to kill her in return.

A few months ago, we were enduring one of these storms of rage and grief, when she suddenly stopped, brought her hands to her face, and in despair, she said, "I am in the mind of my mother!" When I asked what she meant by that, she said, "All this is not me. I feel that I'm trapped inside my mother's mind and can't get out."

This woman professes hate for her mother. In fact, part of her suffering is that she is exhausted by the persistent rage she feels at her long-dead mother. Her earliest memory is of her mother telling her she deserved nothing. She reports that her mother regularly beat her. She had to earn her keep by doing housework and cooking meals for all her younger brothers. This wicked mother was so obsessed with her own anxieties and worries that she had no interest in my patient's thoughts or feelings; indeed, when the patient entered treatment, she had difficulty talking, claiming she had no thoughts or feelings at all.

If I looked at this case from an object-relations perspective, I would see this woman's anxiety as a result of her early interaction with the toxic parent, and focus the treatment on recovering traumatic memories of her relationship to her mother. And indeed for much of the treatment, my patient has talked about her horrible childhood and the abuse and neglect of her mother.

It is interesting to me, though, that although consciously this woman expresses nothing but aggression toward the mother, she seems to be telling me that she can only experience reality from her mother's point of view. Unconsciously, she remains deeply connected to the hated object in a reenactment of the mother's worldview and wishes. Though she sees herself as a victim, in the treatment she is as torturing to herself and to me as her mother was to her.

Thinking about the patient's idea of being "trapped in the mind of my mother" got me listening in a new way to the various stories of how patients process experience in the here and now. I begin to see that many of the people I work with cling to a rigid way of thinking that has very little to do with their actual situation.

There is the beautiful and privileged woman who has a loving, successful husband, two bright, healthy children, and a great talent as a singer who says, "The world is shitty, and I am shitty, and nothing ever turns out right for me." She experiences life as a "tedious ordeal." If her son gets into an Ivy League college, she is miserable because "it wasn't the right one." If she gets praise for her singing, she says, "people are trying to put pressure on me to do something about it, and I know that nothing I can do will ever get me noticed as a singer." Though she is constantly going to lunches and dinners, to shop and play tennis, she says, "I have no friends. At least no real friends. How can I? People are horrible." For this lucky woman, it's as though the world and everything in it, including herself, is a sewer.

I get the idea when I am with her that all the bleakness she brings into my office serves as a protective device, a way to keep herself away from me. When she occasionally reports that something good actually happened, she speaks reluctantly and warily, as if I may punish her for feeling happy or important, even for a moment. Once when she told me that a friend wanted to host an evening so that my patient could showcase her singing, she paused and said, "Is that all right? It's okay, isn't it?"

This woman is one of three sisters, the middle child. Her mother told her daughters that she had never wanted children. She was very uncomfortable as a mother. She particularly disliked and blamed my patient for all the squabbles among the sisters. My patient said, "She liked my oldest sister best because she had a learning disability and suffered a lot. She was comfortable when we were suffering, but none of us were supposed to have anything. We were all supposed to be as miserable as she is. And she made sure that the three of us hated each other."

Now in the treatment room, I feel we are in the mind of the mother; she suffers so I won't kill her.

Another female patient is anxious all the time. She wakes in the night and worries for several hours. She says, "I can attach the anxiety to anything—my son's midterms, my daughter's car trip in the snow. If I'm in a plane, it's going to crash. If I'm in a high-rise building, there will be a bomb. If I have a headache, it's a brain tumor. The idea doesn't really matter. It's the anxiety that's important. It's where I live." She distracts her mind by being a perfectionist and a "worker bee." She gives dinner parties, but doesn't really enjoy them because they have to be "absolutely flawless." She counts the tomato slices as she cuts them and the dishes as they come out of the dishwasher to distract herself from the tension she feels.

She too likes to tell me about her difficult mother. "She was anxious and manicky, like an eddy that sucked everything into it. I am just like her, and I hate it." Her mother spent hours cooking complicated, wonderful food to feed her family—but she tortured everyone with her obsessive desire to make it perfect. She constantly watched my patient for signs of illness or sloppiness, tugging at her hair or feeling her forehead for fever. My patient's first memory is of trying to arrange a blanket for her doll and not being able to "make it perfect." She said to her mother, "Mommy, make it right." Her mother tried anxiously to get the blanket just so, but when she couldn't arrange it perfectly, my patient started to cry, and the mother said in exasperation, "Oh for heaven's sake! Don't be such a perfectionist! You are too melodramatic!" "This," my patient said wryly, "was the pot calling the kettle black."

In the treatment, this woman wants me to feed her as her mother fed her. The food must be delicious. I am supposed to make things perfect—"get it right." The patient came in one day having read about the concept of a stimulus barrier. "I need one of those," she demanded, "Tell me how to get one!" I told her she needs to keep talking. She said, "I don't want to talk. I want to work! Tell me what to do, and I'll do it." She anxiously scrutinizes me as her mother scrutinized her. What do I really think of her? Do I know something I'm not telling her? What does she think of my hair, my clothes? She tries to perfect me by suggesting I cut my hair or change my outfit.

One day when she was particularly exhausted by her own angst, I asked her what I could do to soothe her. She said, "Soothe me? I don't want to be soothed! If you said something to get me to feel less anxious, do you know what would happen? I would walk out of this session feeling happy and calm, get in the elevator, go down to the street and bam! A taxi would hit me and kill me. This anxiety is keeping me alive!"

Yet another patient, a woman who is a rabbi, sees life as a constant struggle between domination and humiliation. Not surprisingly, since she is the youngest of seven sisters, she obsessively feels "left behind and put down" by every object and situation. She watched her overwhelmed mother beat her older sisters, a fate she escaped by being "very, very good." Though she is afraid of her own aggression and still wants desperately to "be good," she constantly fantasizes about beating me (the analyst) and everyone else when she feels she has been slighted in any way. Her fears feel "very strong, very primitive" to her. After several years in analysis, she decided to try to have the fantasy of giving up her terror of being "disrespected." On the way to our session, she invited herself to fantasize a world where she simply put that fear aside. "But when I did," she reported, "my mind crashed." I asked her what she meant by that. She said, "I felt paralyzed, rigid. My mind was empty. I couldn't or wouldn't even fantasize about it." I said, "Sounds like there's something dangerous about giving it up." She stared blankly, "I didn't feel I was in danger," she said, "I just felt sort of dead."

This refusal to even consider a world that doesn't conform to the rigid personal fantasy is very common. My anxious patient said, "I wish I could stop worrying, just give up the constant anxiety, put it down like a heavy package. It's so exhausting and really, it makes my life a living hell. But I can't give it up. Something bad will happen if I do."

Meadow (1989b) talked about the fantasies of the external world that patients create. These fantasies, which form the structure of the patient's ego, are constructed in the pre-object state from pieces of the self—wishes, impulses, primitive defenses, and impressions of the surroundings. When these fantasies override reality, the circuits are closed, going around the same track; the patient is unable to experience anything truly new.

According to Meadow (1996), when we work with patients who are regressed to primitive states, we recognize that something is being protected, and that something is more important than life itself. These primitive fantasies are so rigid and so important because they are the bedrock on which the developing ego rests. They contain the patient's sense of "me-ness," so that to give them up is equivalent to psychic death.

We can think of these inflexible ways of processing stimuli as a response to toxic objects, and certainly getting a patient's history gives us vital information about how the past gets acted out in the present of the session. We need to hear about all these difficult mothers and terrible childhoods if we are to understand the people we work with. And yet, it is not enough. Some of these patients I have described are those whom I have worked with for many years. I have helped them talk about their memories and their histories. Certainly, the patient gains insight in this process, but the rigid mindset that is used to view the world remains unyielding. My perfectionist patient described her persistent anxiety occurring on a "cellular level. It feels genetic rather than psychic."

These primitive fantasies that my patient described as being "in the mind of my mother" are set down very early in life. Indeed, being in the mind of the mother is a dynamic that is probably established when the patient is literally in the body of the mother; that is to say, in intrauterine life.

Piontelli (1992) used the technology of sonography to study fetuses in utero. She then followed these subjects through birth and the first three years of life. Studying the images of babies in their mother's wombs, she discovered that from the moment the fetus begins to have sensory experience, it seems to show highly individualized preferences and reactions. At the least, it seems to be acting on a pleasure/nonpleasure basis. Chamberlain (1983) concurred that all human senses are operative by some time in the second trimester of pregnancy. By the twenty-eighth week of pregnancy, the brain's neural circuits are as advanced as a newborn's, and at about the same time, the cerebral cortex matures enough to support consciousness (Purpora 1975).

Piontelli observed that there is a remarkable consistency between behavior before and after birth, and that many small children show signs after birth of being influenced by experiences they had in the womb. Although infants don't have the developed brain function to "remember" prenatal life, the uterine experience is constantly relived and reworked as they grow and develop. Piontelli's work argues for the possibility that certain pathological and defensive formations may start to develop in the womb.

What my patient calls "genetic" may in fact have its origins in the prenatal, or in the varied elements and stimuli belonging to what Piontelli (37) called "the far from neutral intrauterine environment." Science tells us that physical illness, emotions, states of anxiety or depression, and even negative thinking can effect changes in the chemistry of the body and its fluids. Verny (1981) described the intricate neuron-hormonal loops that link a mother to her unborn child. Anxiety, rage, or depression alter the production of neuron-hormones such as adrenaline, noradrenaline, serotonin, and oxytocin in the mother, and this can significantly alter the body chemistry of the fetus. The actual physical changes that emotions produce are controlled by the hypothalamus and are created in the endocrine and autonomic nervous system. An alteration in these emotional processing centers can mean that the fetus's hypothalamus will be set too low or too high, creating a physical propensity for anxiety, rage, or depression.

Nowhere is self–object merger so complete as in utero. Verny (1981) cited studies that demonstrate that a fraction of a second after fear or anxiety has set a pregnant woman's heart racing, the fetus's heart begins pumping at twice its normal rate. The amniotic environment, so susceptible to influence by the feelings of the mother, is in essence the first "pre-object" the fetus encounters. The fluids pulsing through the placenta are literally the stuff from which the cells of the infant's mind and body develop.

Analysts have long been interested in this primitive merger, the time in every new human being's life when "the same soul governs two bodies" (Leonardo Da Vinci). As early as 1923, Freud talked about a primary identification that is direct and immediate and which takes place before there is an awareness of any object with which to cathect. Beginning in the 1940s and 1950s, analysts such as Klein, Winnicott, and Spotnitz began to emphasize the importance of the initial period of human development, namely uterine, even cellular memory, and the first two years of life. Spotnitz (1987) described the regression that patients in analysis make to an undifferentiated state of development, where the earliest self-representations and object-representations overlap.

Meadow (1981, 208) wrote extensively about this regression where "images in the mind are the real world, and actual people are shadows of those images." In the pre-self–object merged state, there are no clearly perceived objects. Thinking is done through reprocessing internalized visual and auditory impressions and bodily sensations. In this state, the whole world is created and perceived through the lens of our conflicts. The object world (Meadow 1987) is shaped in the image of the patient's pre-object life. Life for the patient is like a stage on which certain dramas are acted out repetitively.

Primitive impressions that dominate the patient's worldview can't be given up, because it means disintegration of the ego.

Recently, neurological science has been catching up with modern analytic ideas in several interesting ways. The importance of pre-language psychic development, and the learning that occurs in self–object merger and undifferentiated states that modern analysts have always emphasized, is now being documented in the neurological laboratory. A recent article in the journal *Nature* (Etcoff et al. 2000) described a study of adults with aphasia, which is the loss of speech, language, and sometimes coherent thought, in people who have suffered stroke or brain damage. The authors found that aphasics have an uncanny ability to detect other people's feelings, particularly lies about emotions. They read nonverbal clues significantly better than did the people with no language impairment. This empathetic skill takes time to develop. People who have been aphasic for only a few months don't seem to have it. The study argued that the loss of language heightened the brain's ability to read other people's minds. Language is intimately tied with cognitive thinking but in its absence, a more primitive form of perception and awareness of the surroundings, a primal reading of the object's mind, seems to flourish. This precognitive absorption of the other describes the world of the fetus and the infant.

The discovery of mirror neurons is another instance of neurological study confirming modern analytic principles. Scientists (Sylwester 2002) have recently been able to observe that the neurons in the pre-motor cortex area that fire perception for upcoming movements also fire when we observe someone else carry out that action. Common brain regions thus process both the perception and production of a movement. In short, watching and doing fire the same brain cells. Mirror neuron activity is thought to control our ability to be empathetic.

Gallese (2004) went even farther to say that the same neural circuits involved in experiencing emotions and sensations are also active when witnessing emotions and sensations in others. To perceive an emotion is equivalent to internally stimulating it. This enables the observer to use her own resources to experientially penetrate the world of the other by means of a direct, automatic, and unconscious process of what Gallese called "embodied simulation." The first- and third-person experience of a given emotion are underpinned by a shared neural substrate. Embodied simulation allows the other's emotion to be constituted, experienced, and directly understood. This is not a willed, cognitive act but is a basic functional mechanism of the brain. By means of a shared neural state realized in two different bodies that nevertheless obey the same morpho-functional rule, the other literally becomes the self.

The studies of aphasics and mirror neurons lend credence to the idea that the preverbal infant has a heightened aptitude in becoming "the mind of the mother." As Meadow (1989a) argued, the human infant has a remarkable need and ability to encompass all around him as a part of himself. Whether that "all around him" is the amniotic fluid and placenta in utero or the breast and face of the mother after birth, the neonate is neurologically wired to read and absorb the mind of the mother.

Living in the mind of the mother is set down in the earliest stages of life, long before there is any awareness of an object perceived as separate from the self. The dynamic is not susceptible to change by a focus on an actual object, toxic or otherwise, or on the realistic environment. It feels "cellular" because the cells were literally formed out of the soma and psyche of the mother.

In 1946, Melanie Klein hypothesized that the first sense of self occurs when the infant can externalize dangerous impulses that threaten to overwhelm the budding ego. Patients create a world image containing parts of the self that are unacceptable. Hateful intrapsychic images can be dealt with, as my singer-patient deals with them, by assuming the world is a hateful place. Klein (1957) and Ogden (1979) described how unacceptable impulses and parts of the self-concept are projected into the mother, and that this process occurs before the identification with mother is established. Meadow (1987; 1991) elaborated on this process by asserting that the object world is created in the image of the patient through projection of unacceptable impulses. The patient's process of separation into a self and other becomes one in which destructive urges must first be perceived as coming from outside his own psyche. The first rumblings of a wish to live, seen in strivings for an object world, are the search for an external port for impulse discharge (Meadow 1989a).

In thinking about my patient with the anxiety attacks from this perspective, I begin to understand the usefulness of seeing the world from the point of view of a helpless victim. If she is her mother's victim, then the aggression is in the mother, not in her. The aggression involved in torturing herself is not hers; it is the mother's. She doesn't see yet that the aggression is her own; in unconscious identification with the mother, she uses it to torture herself (and me) as the mother tortured her. When we are in "the mind of my mother," libido is expressed in the unconscious identification with the mother, and aggression is projected into the mother and then turned against the self.

My patient with the singing talent projects her aggression into me, seeing me as a murderous mother who is unhappy when anything good happens to her and who has to be appeased and controlled by a lifetime of suffering. The woman who gives perfect dinner parties tortures herself with the anxiety that she attributes to her mother, but it is she, in unconscious collusion with the preverbal mother, who inflicts torture of the self in the here and now.

The state of being in the mind of the mother is laid down in the psyche before the first attempts to project aggression out into the object world, but it sets up the conditions that allow this projection. If the patient is in the mind of the mother, they are merged; there is no object. It is this primal fantasy of union that allows the next developmental step of the projection of aggressive impulses into the mother. *If mother and I are one, then my aggression is hers*. The early struggle for an ego projects aggression onto the mother and then sets up a merger/identification with the toxic mother.

Meadow (1981), applying the concept of tension regulation, recommended that we observe how each patient maintains psychic stability. Patients are biological creatures responding to an environment with two sets of drives, and it is important that we not lose sight of the uniqueness of each person's internal balance of the forces of Eros and Thanatos (Meadow 2000). Working with the drive states of narcissistic patients can show the analyst how each person constructed a world and an ego based on impressions before language and before self and object could be perceived as different (Meadow 1989a).

What is crucial to remember in all of this is: The repetitive, rigid way of thinking, believing, and acting, which my patient called being in the mind of the mother, is alive in the here and now of the session, if for no other reason than because the patient who is here in the session was, indeed, created out of the mind of the mother. That patient brings to each meeting a repetition of preverbal experience that was, is now, and will always be the way the patient sees and deals with the world. Patients can deepen the analyst's understanding of dynamics by educating her about the past, but studying the way each person processes stimulation in the moment of the session is the real meat and potatoes of analysis. The repetition compulsion will ensure that repressed impressions and experiences will repeat themselves in the room with the analyst (Meadow 1994). Understanding how the patient repeats the mind of the mother in the transference will lead to a richer understanding of the patient's perception of the past.

The earliest longings and motives of the preverbal patient occurred in a dyad, not the triad of the Oedipal period (Meadow 2000), and those same longings and motives reawaken in the dyad of analysis. The analyst learns about early object patterns by experiencing the feelings of the patient's parents, thereby understanding the feelings the patient was subjected to early in life (Meadow 1989b). The distorted view of reality, which is being in the mind of the mother, like any resistance, must be protected and joined. Psychoanalysis becomes too dangerous to the patient if he believes that the analyst is attempting to deprive him of the way he sees himself in the world. The mind of the mother creates psychic stability and cannot be relinquished.

In the analytic process, each therapist is limited by her own early perceptions of the world. The analyst can also be in the mind of *her* mother, and this means the patient is not always seen clearly, but rather through the lens of the analyst's own distortions of reality (Meadow 1987).

So what can we do to "cure" patients of this dynamic that is so early that it feels *cellular* or *genetic*? More importantly, do we want to free our patients from the mind of the mother? They seem to be telling us they need to be locked in the prison of rigid patterns and thinking or they will come apart. The magnitude and depth of this conundrum is perhaps why Freud became so pessimistic about the ability of psychoanalysis to cure.

A patient recently told me, after years of analysis, that she came into the process hoping I would take away her pain, resolve her "issues," and release her as a cured and happy person. "Instead," she said, "all that has happened is that I understand and can manage my crazy feelings better." She smiled and then added, "And sometimes even enjoy them."

My patient with anxiety attacks has recently been able to sometimes stop the downward spiral of panic and rage at the beginning of the attack. I had suggested to her that, when she felt a spell coming on, she should stop and try to figure out who she is angry at. She has never reported trying that technique, but she did tell me afterward that she has begun to be able to "get a little bit above myself and watch myself have all those horrible feelings, and somehow that gives me a control I didn't used to have."

I need another thirty years of research with people to decide if the mind of the mother can be changed. I believe my patients when they say they need their personal fantasies to survive, so I don't currently work with the goal of getting them to give them up. I could, of course, change my mind (or should I say the mind of my mother) about that as I learn more. As Spotnitz likes to say, "More study is needed."

One goal of psychoanalysis is to help the patient enter the mind of the analyst in a therapeutic way to create new intrapsychic structures. This process is facilitated by developing and then resolving the narcissistic transference. Techniques used by modern analysts that go beyond interpretation, such as joining, mirroring, and reflecting, encourage the narcissistic transference and aid the restructuring of the mind by giving the patient the idea that the analyst and she are of one mind. Meadow (1987) described a woman who had a great desire to be the analyst, to be in her uterus, for the analyst to be in her. In this pre-object state, she was unable to give up the primitive impressions that dominated her inner world. I see this woman's longings as a wish to return to the place where the mind of the mother was imposed on the psyche to begin again with a different kind of mother.

In resolving the narcissistic transference, the analyst must become not only the toxic mother but also the provider of a corrective emotional experience. After the narcissistic transference has been worked through, patients have to give up the infantile desire for unity and bliss, and they need a good and steady object with whom to identify. The analyst must weather the conflict between vacillating negative self and object impressions and the rage generated by the loss of the hope for merger.

Patients want to changes their feelings in analysis but this doesn't usually happen. Instead, the patient changes his mind. The feelings are the expression of the mind of the mother, the earliest impressions created at a cellular level and mistaken from that time forward for reality. Giving them up would mean coming apart, mentally and probably physically. So, the patient mustn't give up the feelings. She needs them to stay alive; they are a survival mechanism.

References

Introduction

Benjamin, J. (1988). *The Bonds of Love: Psychoanalysis, Feminism, and the Problem of Domination*. New York: Pantheon Books.

Bibring, G. L., et al. (1961). "A study of psychological processes in pregnancy and of the earliest mother-child relationship." *Psychoanalytic Study of the Child* 16: 9–72.

Bollas, C. (1992). *Being a Character: Psychoanalysis and Self Experience*. New York: Hill and Wang.

Chodorow, N. (1978). *The Reproduction of Mothering: Psychoanalysis and the Sociology of Gender*. Berkeley: University of California Press.

de Beauvoir, S. (1952). *The Second Sex*. New York: Alfred A. Knopf.

Deutsch, H. (1944, 1945). *The Psychology of Women, Volumes 1 and 2*. New York: Grune and Stratton.

Freud, S. (1908). "On the sexual theories of children." *Standard Edition, Volume 9*. London: Hogarth Press, 205–26.

———. (1924). "The dissolution of the Oedipus complex." *Standard Edition, Volume 19*. London: Hogarth Press, 173–82.

———. (1926). "The question of lay analysis." *Standard Edition, Volume 20*. London: Hogarth Press, 179–258.

———. (1931). "Female sexuality." *Standard Edition, Volume 21*. London: Hogarth Press, 223–46.

———. (1932). "Femininity." *Standard Edition, Volume 22*. London: Hogarth Press, 112–35.

———. (1933). "New introductory lectures on psychoanalysis." *Standard Edition, Volume 22*. London: Hogarth Press, 3–184.

Gilligan, C. (1982). *In a Different Voice: Psychological Theory and Women's Development*. Cambridge, MA: Harvard University Press.
Mackay, N. (1989). *Motivation and Explanation*. Madison, CT: International Universities Press.
Miller, J. B. (1976). *Toward A New Psychology of Women*. Boston: Beacon Press.
Montgrain, N. (January 1, 1983). "On the vicissitudes of female sexuality: The difficult path from anatomical destiny to psychic representation." *International Journal of Psychoanalysis* 64: 69–119.

Chapter 1

Becker, T. E. (1974). "On Latency." *Psychoanalytic Study of the Child* 29: 3–12.
Benjamin, J. (1988). *The Bonds of Love: Psychoanalysis, Feminism, and the Problem of Domination*. New York: Pantheon Books.
Blos, P. (1958). "Pre-adolescent drive organization." *JAPA* 6: 47–56.
———. (1976). "When and how does adolescence end? Structural criteria for adolescent closure." *Adolescent Psychiatry, Volume 5*, edited by S. C. Feinstein and P. Giovacchini. New York: Jason Aronson.
Bonaparte, M. (1951). *Female Sexuality*. Madison, CT: International Universities Press.
Chasseguet-Smirgel, J. (1970). *Female Sexuality: New Psychoanalytic Views*. London: Karnac Books.
Chodorow, N. (1978). *The Reproduction of Mothering: Psychoanalysis and the Sociology of Gender*. Berkeley: University of California Press.
Crowell, M. G. (1981). "A response to feminist critics of psychoanalysis." *Modern Psychoanalysis* 6: 221–35.
de Beauvoir, S. (1952). *The Second Sex*. New York: Alfred A. Knopf.
Deutsch, H. (1944, 1945). *The Psychology of Women, Volumes 1 and 2*. New York: Grune and Stratton.
Dinnerstein, D. (1976). *The Mermaid and the Minotaur: Sexual Arrangements and Human Malaise*. New York: HarperCollins.
Ernsberger, C. (1976). "Freud and the modern school." *Modern Psychoanalysis* 1: 17–32.
Freud, S. (1905). "Three essays on the theory of sexuality." *Standard Edition, Volume 7*. London: Hogarth Press, 125–248.
———. (1924). "The dissolution of the Oedipus complex." *Standard Edition, Volume 19*. London: Hogarth Press, 173–82.
———. (1925). "Some psychical consequences of the anatomical distinction between the sexes." *Standard Edition, Volume 19*. London: Hogarth Press, 243–60.
———. (1931). "Female sexuality." *Standard Edition, Volume 21*. London: Hogarth Press, 223–46.
———. (1932). "Femininity." *Standard Edition, Volume 22*. London: Hogarth Press, 112–35.

———. (1933). "New introductory lectures on psychoanalysis." *Standard Edition, Volume 22*. London: Hogarth Press, 3–184.

Gilligan, C. (1982) *In a Different Voice: Psychological Theory and Women's Development*. Cambridge, MA: Harvard University Press.

———. N. P. Lyons, and T. J. Hanmer, eds. (1989). *Making Connections: The Relational Worlds of Adolescent Girls at Emma Willard School*. Cambridge, MA: Harvard University Press.

Horney, K. (1967). *Feminine Psychology*. New York: W. W. Norton and Company.

Jacobson, E. (1961). "Adolescent moods and the remodeling of psychic structures in adolescence." *Psychoanalytic Study of the Child* 16: 164–83.

Jones, E. (1927). "The early development of female sexuality." *International Journal of Psychoanalysis* 8: 459–72.

———. (1935). "Early female sexuality." *International Journal of Psychoanalysis* 16: 263–73.

Klein, M., and Riviere, J. (1964). *Love, Hate, and Reparation*. New York: W. W. Norton.

Spotnitz, H. (1964). "Adolescence and schizophrenia: Problems in differentiation." *Adolescents: Psychoanalytic Approach to Problems and Therapy*, edited by S. Lorand and H. I. Scheer. New York: Harper and Row.

Chapter 2

Benjamin, J. (1988). *The Bonds of Love: Psychoanalysis, Feminism, and the Problem of Domination*. New York: Pantheon Books.

Bibring, G. L., et al. (1961). "A study of psychological processes in pregnancy and of the earliest mother-child relationship." *Psychoanalytic Study of the Child* 16: 9–72.

Chodorow, N. (1978). *The Reproduction of Mothering: Psychoanalysis and the Sociology of Gender*. Berkeley: University of California Press.

Crowell, M. G. (1981). "A response to feminist critics of psychoanalysis." *Modern Psychoanalysis* 6: 221–35.

Davis, E. (1985). *The Role of Aggression in the Psychobiology of Pregnancy and Infertility*. Cincinnati: Union Institute P.D.E.

de Beauvoir, S. (1952). *The Second Sex*. New York: Alfred A. Knopf.

Deutsch, H. (1944, 1945). *The Psychology of Women, Volumes 1 and 2*. New York: Grune and Stratton.

Freud, S. (1931). "Female sexuality." *Standard Edition, Volume 21*. London: Hogarth Press, 223–46.

———. (1932). "Femininity." *Standard Edition, Volume 22*. London: Hogarth Press, 112–35.

Horney, K. (1967). *Feminine Psychology*. New York: W. W. Norton and Company.

Klein, M. and Riviere, J. (1964). *Love, Hate, and Reparation*. New York: W. W. Norton.

Langer, M. (1992). *Motherhood and Sexuality*. New York: The Guilford Press.

Loewald, H. (1962). "Internalization, separation, mourning, and the super ego." *Psychoanalytic Quarterly* 31: 483–504.

Mitchell, J. (1974). *Psychoanalysis and Feminism: Freud, Reich, Laing, and Women*. New York: Vintage Books.

Piontelli, A. (1992). *From Fetus to Child: An Observational and Psychoanalytic Study*. London: Tavistock/Routledge.

Rabuzzi, K. (1994). *Mother with Child: Transformations Through Childbirth*. Bloomington: Indiana University Press.

Rich, A. (1976). *Of Woman Born: Motherhood as Experience and Institution*. New York: W. W. Norton and Company.

Spotnitz, H., and Freeman, L. (1969). *How to be Happy though Pregnant*. New York: Berkley Publishing Corporation.

Chapter 3

Bemesderfer. S. (1996). "A revised psychoanalytic view of menopause." *Journal of the American Psychoanalytic Association* 44: 351–72, 631–38.

Benedek, T. (1950). "Climacterium: A developmental phase." *Psychoanalytic Quarterly* 19: 1–27.

Clevens, E. (1976). "The depressive reaction." *Modern Psychoanalysis* 1, no. 2: 139–47.

Deutsch, H. (1924). "The menopause." *International Journal of Psychoanalysis* 65, no. 1: 56.

———. (1945). "The climacterium." *The Psychology of Women: A Psychoanalytic Interpretation, Volume 2*. New York; Grune and Stratton, 456–87.

Freud, S. (1905). "On psychotherapy." *Standard Edition, Volume 7*. London: Hogarth Press, 257–68.

———. (1912). "Types of onset of neurosis." *Standard Edition, Volume 12*. London: Hogarth Press, 227–38.

———. (1913). "The disposition to obsessional neurosis." *Standard Edition, Volume 12*. London: Hogarth Press, 311–26.

———. (1917). "Mourning and melancholia." *Standard Edition, Volume 14*. London: Hogarth Press, 237–60.

———. (1917). "Anxiety." *Standard Edition, Volume 16*. London: Hogarth Press, 392–411.

———. (1926). "The question of lay analysis." *Standard Edition, Volume 20*. London: Hogarth Press, 179–258.

———. (1933). "New introductory lectures on psychoanalysis." *Standard Edition, Volume 22*. London: Hogarth Press, 3–184.

Greer, G. (1991). *The Change: Women, Aging and the Menopause*. New York: Fawcett Columbine.

Klein, M. (1932). *The Psychoanalysis of Children*, 232–33.

Chapter 4

Atwood, G. E., and Stolorow, R. D. (1999). *Faces in a Cloud: Intersubjectivity in Personality Theory*. Northvale, NJ: Jason Aronson.

Breger, L. (1981). *Freud's Unfinished Journey: Conventional and Critical Perspectives in Psychoanalytic Theory*. London: Routledge and Kegan Paul.

Bollas, C. (1987). *The Shadow of the Object*. New York: Columbia University Press.

Foxe, G. (1995). "Anorexia as characterological metaphor." *Modern Psychoanalysis* 20, no. 2, 131–51.

Freud, S. (1926). "The question of lay analysis." *Standard Edition, Volume 20*. London: Hogarth Press, 179–258.

———. (1932). "Femininity." *Standard Edition, Volume 22*. London: Hogarth Press, 112–35.

Gay, P. (1988). *Freud: A Life for our Times*. New York: W. W. Norton and Company.

Hoffman, L. (1996). "Freud and feminine subjectivity." *JAPA* 44, supplement: 23–44.

Margolis, B. (1994). "Treatment and transition: observations on modern psychoanalysis." *Modern Psychoanalysis* 19, no. 2, 227–40.

Meadow, P. (2000). "Creating psychic change in analysis." *Modern Psychoanalysis* 25, no. 1: 3–22.

Rosaldo, M. Z., and Lamphere, L., eds. (1974). *Woman, Culture and Society*. Stanford, CA: Stanford University Press.

Spotnitz, H., and Meadow P. (1976). *Treatment of the Narcissistic Neurosis*. New York: Manhattan Center for Advanced Group Studies.

Chapter 5

Bollas, C. (1992). *Being A Character*. New York: Hill and Wang.

Chodorow, N. (1978). *The Reproduction of Mothering: Psychoanalysis and the Sociology of Gender*. Berkeley: University of California Press.

de Beauvoir, S. (1952). *The Second Sex*. New York: Alfred A. Knopf.

Freud, S. (1925). "Some psychical consequences of the anatomical distinction between the sexes." *Standard Edition, Volume 19*. London: Hogarth Press, 243–60.

Gilligan, C., et al. eds. (1989). *Making Connections: The Relational World of Adolescent Girls at Emma Willard School*. Cambridge, MA: Harvard University Press.

Holmes, L. (2000). "The internal triangle: New theories of female development. *Modern Psychoanalysis*, 25: 207–226.

Miller, J. B. (1976). *Toward A New Psychology of Women*. Boston: Beacon Press.

Ormont, L. R. (1990). The craft of bridging. *International Journal of Group Psychotherapy*, 40:1, 5–30.

———. (1991). *The Group Therapy Experience*. New York: St. Martin's Press.

Chapter 6

Bollas, C. (1987). *The Shadow of the Object: Psychoanalysis of the Unthought Known.* New York: Columbia University Press.

———. (1992). *Being A Character: Psychoanalysis and Self Experience.* New York: Hill and Wang.

Chodorow, N. (1999). *The Power of Feelings: Personal Meaning in Psychoanalysis, Gender, and Culture.* New Haven, CT: Yale University Press.

Freud, A. (1960). "Entrance into nursery school: The psychological prerequisites." *The Writings of Anna Freud, Volume 5.* New York: International Universities Press, 315–35.

———. (1965). *Normality and Pathology in Childhood: Assessments of Development.* New York: International Universities Press.

Freud, S. (1905). "Jokes and their relation to the unconscious." *Standard Edition, Volume 8.* London: Hogarth Press, 3–248.

Kaplan H., and Sadock, B. (1981). *Modern Synopsis of Comprehensive Textbook of Psychiatry, III.* Baltimore: Williams and Wilkins.

Livingston, M. (2001). "Self psychology, dreams and group psychotherapy: Working in the playspace." *Group* 25, nos. 1/2: 15–26.

Ormont, L. (1997). "Bridging in group analysis." *Modern Psychoanalysis* 22, no. 1: 59–77.

———. (2001). "Resolving resistances to immediacy in the group." *The Technique of Group Treatment.* Madison, CT: Psychosocial Press, 103–22.

———. (2001). "Progressive emotional communication: Criteria for a well-functioning group." *The Technique of Group Treatment.* Madison, CT: Psychosocial Press, 373–83.

Winnicott, D.W. (1953). "Transitional objects and transitional phenomena: A study of the first not-me possession." *International Journal of Psychoanalysis* 43: 89–97.

———. (1964). "Why children play." *The Child, the Family, and the Outside World.* Middlesex, England: Penguin Books, 143–46.

———. (1971). "Playing: A theoretical statement." *Playing and Reality.* London: Tavistock.

———. (1989). *Psychoanalytic Explorations.* Cambridge, MA: Harvard University Press, 28–29, 59–63, 203–6.

Chapter 7

Holmes, L. (2000). "The internal triangle: new theories of female development." *Modern Psychoanalysis* 25: 207–26.

Chapter 8

Chamberlain, D. B. (1983). *Consciousness at Birth: A Review of the Empirical Evidence.* San Diego, CA: Chamberlain Publications.

Etcoff, N., et al. (2000). "Lie detection and language comprehension." *Nature* 405: 139.

Gallese, V. (2004). "Intentional attunement, the mirror neuron system and its role in interrelations." *European Science Foundation*.

Klein, M. (1946). "Notes on schizoid mechanisms." *Developments in Psychoanalysis*, edited by Joan Riviere. New York: Da Capo Press, 1983, 292–320.

Klein M. (1957). *Envy and Gratitude*. New York: W.W. Norton and Co.

Leonardo da Vinci. *Quaderni*.

Meadow, P.W. (1981). "Drive theory in diagnosis and treatment." *Modern Psychoanalysis* 6, no. 2, 141–70.

———. (1987). "The myth of the impersonal analyst." *Modern Psychoanalysis* 12, no. 2: 131–50.

———. (1989a). "Object relations in a drive theory model." *Modern Psychoanalysis* 14, no. 1, 57–74.

———. (1989b). "How we aim to be with patients." *Modern Psychoanalysis* 14, no. 2, 145–62.

———. (1991). "Resonating with the psychotic patient." *Modern Psychoanalysis* 16, no. 1, 87–104.

———. (1994). "The role of aggression in impulse disorders." *Modern Psychoanalysis* 19, no. 1, 27–32.

———. (1996). "The pre-Oedipal transference." *Modern Psychoanalysis* 21, no. 2, 191–200.

———. (2000). "Creating psychic change in analysis." *Modern Psychoanalysis* 25, no. 1, 3–22.

Ogden, T. (1979). "On projective identification." *IJP* 60: 357–73.

Piontelli, A. (1992). *From Fetus to Child: An Observational and Psychoanalytic Study*. London and New York: Tavistock/Routledge.

Purpura, D. (1975). "Consciousness." *Behavior Today* (June 2, 1975): 494.

Spotnitz, H. (1987). *Psychotherapy of Pre-Oedipal Conditions*. Northvale, NJ: Jason Aronson.

Sylwester, R. (2002). "Mirror neurons." *Brain Connection* 181, no. 1.

Verny, T. (1981). *The Secret Life of the Unborn Child*. New York: Dell Publishing.

Index

About the Author

Lucy Holmes is a psychoanalyst in private practice in New York City. She is president of the Society of Modern Psychoanalysts and a member of the faculty at the Center for Modern Psychoanalytic Studies and the Center for Group Studies in New York. She lectures in locations across the country and has published numerous articles on psychoanalysis and female development, one of which, "The Object Within: Childbirth as a Developmental Milestone," won the Gradiva Award for Best Article of 2002, presented by the National Association for the Advancement of Psychoanalysis. This is her first book.

www.ingramcontent.com/pod-product-compliance
Ingram Content Group UK Ltd.
Pitfield, Milton Keynes, MK11 3LW, UK
UKHW012042150926
475560UK00001B/138

9 780765 705495